Best Easy Day Hikes
New River Gorge National Park and Preserve

Help Us Keep This Guide Up to Date

Every effort has been made by the author and editors to make this guide as accurate and useful as possible; however, many things can change after a guide is published—regulations change, facilities come under new management, and so forth.

We would love to hear from you concerning your experiences with this guide and how you feel it could be improved and kept up to date. While we may not be able to respond to all comments and suggestions, we'll take them to heart, and we'll also make certain to share them with the author. Please send your comments and suggestions to falconeditorial@rowman.com.

Thanks for your input!

Best Easy Day Hikes Series

Best Easy Day Hikes New River Gorge National Park and Preserve

Second Edition

Johnny Molloy

FALCONGUIDES

ESSEX, CONNECTICUT

FALCONGUIDES®

An imprint of Globe Pequot, the trade division of The Rowman & Littlefield Publishing Group, Inc.
4501 Forbes Blvd., Ste. 200
Lanham, MD 20706
www.rowman.com

Falcon and FalconGuides are registered trademarks and Make Adventure Your Story is a trademark of The Rowman & Littlefield Publishing Group, Inc.

Distributed by NATIONAL BOOK NETWORK

Copyright © 2023 The Rowman & Littlefield Publishing Group, Inc.

Maps by Melissa Baker and The Rowman & Littlefield Publishing Group, Inc.

British Library Cataloguing in Publication Information available

Library of Congress Cataloging-in-Publication Data available
ISBN 978-1-4930-6751-0 (paper: alk. paper)
ISBN 978-1-4930-6752-7 (electronic)

∞™ The paper used in this publication meets the minimum requirements of American National Standard for Information Sciences—Permanence of Paper for Printed Library Materials, ANSI/NISO Z39.48-1992.

Contents

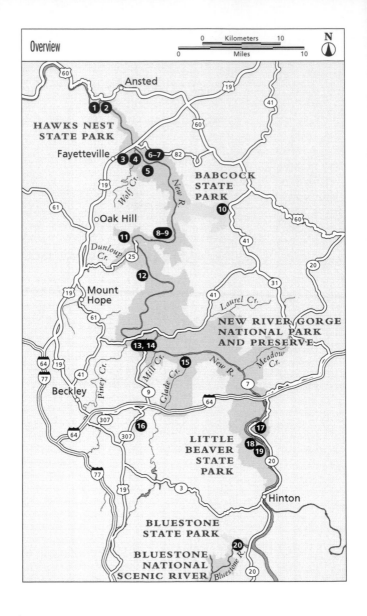

Acknowledgments

Thanks to all the people who helped me with this book, primarily the people at Falcon. Thanks to Sierra Designs for their dry tents, warm jackets, and sturdy packs. Also, thanks to all the park personnel who answered my tireless questions while trying to manage these jewels of the New River Gorge. The biggest thanks go to the local West Virginia hikers and trail builders, as well as those who visit this scenic slice of America, for without y'all there wouldn't be trails in the first place.

Introduction

The astonishing view stretched deep into the gorge. I stood on the sandstone outcrop. Below me flowed the ancient New River, carving an amazing canyon ever deeper. Frothing rapids echoed off the wooded walls that rose from the bottom. The relics of Kaymoor Mine stood across the gorge. The sheer cliff of the Endless Wall stretched to the yon. Diamond Point, but one of many scenic and rewarding destinations in this guide, encapsulated this marvelous parcel of West Virginia. I mentally reflected on other destinations, recounting all the worthwhile hikes at New River Gorge National Park and Preserve.

Established as a national river in 1978, the New River Gorge was rededicated as a national park and preserve in 2020, further cementing its already legendary reputation for beauty and splendor.

To the south, the Bluestone Turnpike led along a designated wild and scenic tributary to a forgotten town. Sandstone Falls brawled its giant river-wide whitewater froth. Gwinn Ridge Trail traversed a lonely ridgetop, where wildlife from bears to deer can be seen. Glade Creek, another tributary of the New River, held towering forests along a trout-rich stream with waterfalls, cascades, and swimming holes. The appropriately named Grandview presented spectacular vistas from the canyon rim and geological formations aplenty. Still other trails led alongside the New River, presenting a serene face in its quiet pools, separated by booming whitewater rapids that drew in kayakers, canoers, and rafters from hundreds of miles. Water accesses were numerous for the gorge hikers, whether on the Stone Cliff Trail, Southside Trail, or others.

Little Beaver was but one of several West Virginia state parks that add quality hikes to this guide. The views from Hawks Nest State Park amazed! The hikes there visited cliffs, boulders, and waterfalls and included a tram ride in season. Babcock State Park contained a hike that started near an interesting gristmill, then climbed to a stone pillar and on to the back of beyond.

And what would the New River Gorge be without coal-mining history? The National Park Service has done a stellar job in preserving this area's past. Visit the townsite of Red Ash, where you can find evidence of its past amid a forest that has reclaimed the site. The Rend Trail traveled an old railroad grade connecting mining facilities. I could see Brooklyn Mine and the closed shaft and nearby ruins. The entire mine and community of Nuttallburg are on the National Register of Historic Places. It has been preserved and enhanced with interpretive information that brings the past to life as you walk through it. The Kaymoor area near Fayetteville has several hikes detailing not only the past but also natural beauty that can be well appreciated from places like Long Point. Here you can also overlook the famed New River Bridge, the largest suspension bridge in the country. The yell of rafters far below Diamond Point brought me back to the here and now. And yes, not only can you hike the New River Gorge but also raft, kayak, camp, climb, and fish. It is truly a national treasure, deserving of its national park status.

With this book in hand and willing feet, you can explore the New River Gorge. No matter where you go, the trails in this book will enhance your outdoor experience and leave you appreciating the natural splendors of West Virginia. Enjoy.

The Nature of the New River Gorge

The New River Gorge's hiking grounds range from single-track wooded tracks along rivers and ridges to well-marked nature trails to strolls on interpretive paths. Hikes in this guide cover the gamut. While by definition a best easy day hike is not strenuous and generally poses little danger to the traveler, knowing a few details about the nature of the New River Gorge will enhance your explorations.

Weather

Southern West Virginia certainly experiences all four seasons. Summer can be warm, with sporadic downright hot spells despite the elevations. Morning hikers can avoid any heat and the common afternoon thunderstorms. Hiking increases when the first northerly fronts of fall sweep cool clear air across the Mountain State. Crisp mornings give way to warm afternoons. Fall is drier than summer. Winter will bring frigid subfreezing days, chilling rains, and significant snow, especially atop the gorge. However, a brisk hiking pace will keep you warm. Each cold month has a few days of mild weather. Make the most of them. Spring will be more variable. A warm day can be followed by a cold snowy one. Extensive spring rains bring regrowth but also keep hikers indoors and flood the New River and its tributaries. But any avid hiker will find more good hiking days than they will have time to hike in spring and every other season.

Critters

New River trail treaders will encounter mostly benign creatures on these trails, such as deer, squirrels, wild turkeys, a variety of songbirds, rabbits, and especially deer. And they can get big here. Don't be surprised to encounter a black bear in the gorge. If you do, simply stand back and let it go its way. Avoid direct eye contact. Most likely the bear will quickly take off from your presence. Never feed a bear under any circumstances. A fed bear is a dead bear. They become food habituated and will do anything to get more of the elixir known as human food. They ultimately get hit by a vehicle, shot, or euthanized. More rarely seen (during the daylight hours especially) are coyotes, raccoons, and opossums. Deer in some of the state parks are remarkably tame and may linger on or close to the trail as you approach. If you feel uncomfortable when encountering any critter, keep your distance and they will generally keep theirs.

Be Prepared

Hiking in the New River Gorge is generally safe. Still, hikers should be prepared, whether they are out for a short stroll at Fayetteville's Town Park or venturing into secluded sections of the gorge. Some specific advice:

- Know the basics of first aid, including how to treat bleeding; bites and stings; and fractures, strains, or sprains. Pack a first-aid kit on each excursion.

- Familiarize yourself with the symptoms of heat exhaustion and heat stroke. Heat exhaustion symptoms include heavy sweating, muscle cramps, headache, dizziness, and fainting. Should you or any of your hiking party exhibit any of these symptoms, cool the victim down immediately by rehydrating and getting the person to an air-conditioned location. Cold showers also help reduce body temperature. Heat stroke is much more serious:

The victim may lose consciousness, and the skin is hot and dry to the touch. In this event, call 911 immediately.

- Regardless of the weather, your body needs a lot of water while hiking. A full thirty-two-ounce bottle is the minimum for these short hikes, but more is always better. Bring a full water bottle, whether water is available along the trail or not.

- Don't drink from streams, rivers, creeks, or lakes without treating or filtering the water first. Waterways and water bodies may host a variety of contaminants, including giardia, which can cause serious intestinal unrest.

- Prepare for extremes of both heat and cold by dressing in layers.

- Carry a backpack in which you can store extra clothing, ample drinking water and food, and whatever extras, such as binoculars, you might want. Consider bringing a GPS with tracking capabilities.

- Cell phone coverage is very limited, but you can never be absolutely sure until you are on location. Atop the Appalachian Plateau near Beckley, Oak Hill, or Fayetteville may yield coverage, but it is almost nonexistent in the gorge depths. Bring your device, but make sure you've turned it off or have it on the vibrate setting while hiking. Nothing like a "wake the dead"–loud ring to startle every creature, including fellow hikers.

- Keep children under careful watch. Trails travel along the New River and its tributaries, most of which are not recommended for swimming. Be watchful along the many overlooks and old mine areas. Hazards along some of the trails include poison ivy, uneven footing, and steep drop-offs; make sure children don't stray from the designated route. Children should carry a plastic whistle; if they become lost, they should stay in one place and blow the whistle to summon help.

Zero Impact

Trails in the greater New River Gorge are well used year-round. We, as trail users, must be especially vigilant to make sure our passage leaves no lasting mark. Here are some basic guidelines for preserving trails in the region. For more information visit www.LNT.org.

- Pack out all your own trash, including biodegradable items, such as orange peels. You might also pack out garbage left by less-considerate hikers.
- Don't approach or feed any wild creatures—the ground squirrel eyeing your snack food is best able to survive if it remains self-reliant.
- Don't pick wildflowers or gather rocks, antlers, feathers, and other treasures along the trail, especially mine and settler relics. Removing these items will only take away from the next hiker's experience and steal a piece of the historic puzzle that is the New River Gorge.
- Avoid damaging trailside soils and plants by remaining on the established route. This is also a good rule of thumb for avoiding poison ivy and other common regional trailside irritants.
- Be courteous by not making loud noises while hiking.
- Many of these trails are multiuse, which means you'll share them with other hikers, trail runners, mountain

bikers, and equestrians. Familiarize yourself with the proper trail etiquette, yielding the trail when appropriate.

- Use outhouses at trailheads or along the trail.

New River Gorge Area Boundaries and Corridors

For the purposes of this guide, best easy day hikes are confined to a one-hour drive from Beckley, West Virginia.

Two major interstates and a major highway converge around the gorge. Directions to trailheads are given from these interstates and other arteries. They include I-64, I-77, and US 19—the divided highway with marked exits that uses the famed New River Bridge to span the river.

Land Management

The following government organizations manage most of the public lands described in this guide and can provide further information on these hikes and other trails in their service areas.

New River Gorge National Park and Preserve, PO Box 246, 104 Main St., Glen Jean, WV 25846; (304) 465-0508; www.nps.gov/neri

West Virginia State Parks, 324 4th Ave., South Charleston, WV 25303; (304) 558-2764; https://wvstateparks.com

How to Use This Guide

This guide is designed to be simple and easy to use. Each hike is described with a map and summary information that delivers the trail's vital statistics, including length, difficulty, fees and permits, park hours, canine compatibility, and trail contacts. Directions to the trailhead are also provided, along with a general description of what you'll see along the way. A detailed route finder (Miles and Directions) sets forth mileages between significant landmarks along the trail.

Hike Selection

This guide describes trails that are accessible to every hiker, whether visiting from out of town or someone lucky enough to live in the New River Gorge area. The hikes are no longer than 6.2 miles round-trip, and most are considerably shorter. They range in difficulty from flat excursions perfect for a family outing to more challenging hilly treks. While these trails are among the best, keep in mind that nearby trails, often in the same park or preserve, may offer options better suited to your needs. I've sought to space hikes throughout the greater New River Gorge region, so wherever your starting point, you'll find a great easy day hike nearby.

Difficulty Ratings

These are all easy hikes, but easy is a relative term. To aid in the selection of a hike that suits particular needs and abilities, each is rated easy, moderate, or more challenging. Bear in mind that even the most challenging routes can be made easy by hiking within your limits and taking rests when you need them.

Easy hikes are generally short and flat, taking no longer than an hour to complete.

Moderate hikes involve increased distance and relatively mild changes in elevation, and will take one to two hours to complete.

More challenging hikes feature some steep stretches, greater distances, and generally take longer than two hours to complete.

These are completely subjective ratings—consider that what you think is easy is entirely dependent on your level of fitness and the adequacy of your gear (primarily shoes). If you are hiking with a group, you should select a hike with a rating that's appropriate for the least fit and prepared in your party.

Approximate hiking times are based on the assumption that on flat ground, most walkers average 2 miles per hour. Adjust that rate by the steepness of the terrain and your level of fitness (subtract time if you're an aerobic animal and add time if you're hiking with kids), and you have a ballpark hiking duration. Be sure to add more time if you plan to picnic or take part in other activities such as bird-watching or photography.

Trail Finder

Best Hikes for River and Stream Lovers

Best Hikes for Children

Best Hikes for Dogs

Best Hikes for Great Views

Best Hikes for Solitude

Best Hikes for History Buffs

Best Hikes for Nature Lovers

Best Hikes for Waterfall Lovers

Map Legend

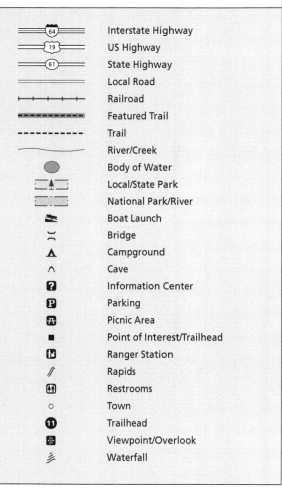

	Interstate Highway
	US Highway
	State Highway
	Local Road
	Railroad
	Featured Trail
	Trail
	River/Creek
	Body of Water
	Local/State Park
	National Park/River
	Boat Launch
	Bridge
	Campground
	Cave
	Information Center
	Parking
	Picnic Area
	Point of Interest/Trailhead
	Ranger Station
	Rapids
	Restrooms
	Town
	Trailhead
	Viewpoint/Overlook
	Waterfall

1 Hawks Nest via Cliff Side Trail

This hike at Hawks Nest State Park joins the base of cliffs overlooking Hawks Nest Lake, a dammed part of the New River. Traverse irregular terrain at the base of this cliff line where you will see huge rock houses, massive boulders, and impressive overhangs. Cruise by the waterfalls of Turkey Creek before climbing back to the gorge rim and enjoying a view from the Hawks Nest, a historic vista that provides an ample reward for your efforts. The irregular footing makes for slow going, but the distance makes it doable by just about everyone.

Distance: 2.6-mile there-and-back

Hiking time: About 2.0 to 3.0 hours

Difficulty: Moderate, does have irregular trail bed

Trail surface: Natural surface

Best season: Year-round, spring for waterfalls

Other trail users: None

Canine compatibility: Leashed dogs permitted

Fees and permits: None

Schedule: Sunrise to sunset

Maps: Hawks Nest State Park Map & Trail Guide; USGS Fayetteville, Beckwith

Trail contacts: Hawks Nest State Park, 49 Hawks Nest Park Rd., Ansted 25812; (304) 658-5212; https://wvstateparks.com/park/hawks-nest-state-park

Finding the trailhead: From the New River Gorge Visitor Center just north of the New River Bridge on US 19, drive north on US 19 for 4.8 miles to the US 60 exit, Hico/Rainelle. Take US 60 west for 7.6 miles to Hawks Nest State Park, passing through the town of Ansted. Enter the park and turn left toward the lodge. Pass the lodge on your left, then immediately look for the Midland Picnic Shelter, below

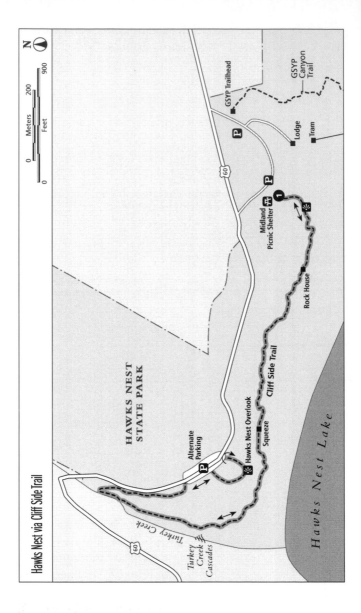

Hawks Nest via Cliff Side Trail

HAWKS NEST
STATE PARK

Turkey Creek
Cascades

Turkey Creek

Alternate
Parking

Hawks Nest Overlook

Squeeze

Cliff Side Trail

Rock House

Midland
Picnic Shelter

Hawks Nest Lake

GSYP Trailhead

GSYP
Canyon
Trail

Lodge

Tram

N

0   Meters   200

0   Feet   900

the park access road on your left. The Cliff Side Trail begins directly behind the picnic shelter. GPS trailhead coordinates: 38.121300, -81.119800

The Hike

The Midland Picnic Shelter makes for a good jumping-off point. It offers shaded picnic tables and a water fountain and is conveniently located at the Cliff Side Trail's eastern terminus. The rocky, rooty trail is bordered by large hardwoods and wastes no time slipping off the gorge rim. A hiking stick will help you keep your balance. The New River lies far below. Interesting rock formations reveal themselves in the adjoining woods—pillars, overhangs, and sheer walls. Your first vista with limited views comes quickly, and then the trail takes you directly underneath an outcrop and you find an overhanging rock house! This is a typical example of the geological Nirvana that lies along this path.

Just a short distance lies between the picnic shelter and the fascinating stonework of the cliffs under which you walk. Immediately pass boulder viewpoints, a narrow trail squeeze, and a huge overhanging rock house. The trail heads westerly along the base of the cliff line. The rock formations rise in a variety of colors, primarily tan, but also gray, brown, and even a greenish tint where moss and lichens have found a home. Navigate around huge boulders that have fallen off the cliff line and landed at its base. The smaller boulders create convenient resting seats.

Undulate along the cliff line. These ups and downs aren't difficult, but the trail rarely stays perfectly level. Aquatic views below will be scattered among the trees in summer but will be more abundant in winter. Make a trail squeeze between boulders and then come to a huge, curved cliff line. After a while the dam of Hawks Nest Lake comes into view. Then you turn from the gorge and enter the moist Turkey Creek watershed. Rhododendron increase in number, as do beech and black birch. Turkey Creek spills in rocky cataracts, creating several attractive water features, highlighted by 18-foot Turkey Creek Cascades.

The path turns away from Turkey Creek and then comes along US 60. Reach a parking area accessible from US 60. Here a wider stone slab trail leaves right to Hawks Nest Overlook. Viewing scopes enhance your ability to see the landscape below. Most visitors will have simply driven to this parking lot, taking the easy way, but you will have truly earned your stripes by reaching the overlook via the Cliff Side Trail. Passersby have been enjoying this overlook for over 200 years. Here you can gaze upstream at the railroad bridge crossing the New River and into the deep wooded canyon. To your right, the Hawks Nest Dam temporarily slows the river, but downriver rapids can be seen below the impoundment. Cliffs and mountains rise across from the overlook, completing the picture.

Miles and Directions

0.0 Pick up the Cliff Side Trail as it heads away from the rear of the Midland Picnic Shelter. Immediately descend on a rocky singletrack path toward the New River. A sign states that children must be accompanied by an adult on the white-blazed trail.

0.1 A short spur trail leads left to a rock outcrop with limited views. Ahead, a set of stairs leads down a break in the cliff line to an overhanging shelter.

0.2 Come to a huge rock house. Its roof stands 40 feet above you and extends several feet back and is completely dry in the rain; I have experienced this.

0.4 Step over a wet-weather stream falling off the canyon rim. Squeeze between boulders.

0.8 Turn away from the New River Gorge into the Turkey Creek valley. Shortly come to Turkey Creek Cascades followed by a host of lesser spillers and slides.

1.0 Walk below the state park entrance sign on US 60.

1.1 Emerge at the Hawks Nest parking area, accessible from US 60. Continue through the lot and then leave right on a stone slab footpath toward Hawks Nest Overlook.

1.2 Reach the overlook, bordered in stone. Viewing scopes allow close looks at the New River Gorge, Hawks Nest Lake, and the rugged lands beyond.

1.3 The walkway emerges at the far end of the US 60 Hawks Nest parking lot. Backtrack.

2.6 Arrive back at the Midland Picnic Shelter and the trailhead, completing the hike.

2 Tram Hike at Hawks Nest State Park

This unusual hike takes place at Hawks Nest State Park. Start out by dropping into the New River Gorge on a steep path to reach the river, at this point dammed as Hawks Nest Lake. Visit the waterside facilities, including a boat dock and nature center, before turning up the Hawks Nest Rail Trail. The rail trail works up the valley of Mill Creek, which spills in pools and cascades, to Fox Branch Falls. Here you will cross some trestles before ending your hike at the site of old Mill Creek Mine. Then backtrack to Hawks Nest Lake. Finally, take the state park tram out of the gorge and back to the park lodge. This makes the hike a lot easier, but be aware the tram has limited operating hours so it's best to call ahead to make sure the tram will be open when you visit. Otherwise, you can hike back out of the gorge on your own.

Distance: 2.4-mile there-and-back with tram ride, 3.2 miles without tram ride
Hiking time: About 2.5 to 3.5 hours
Difficulty: Moderate
Trail surface: Natural surface
Best season: When tram is open
Other trail users: None
Canine compatibility: Leashed dogs permitted

Fees and permits: None
Schedule: Sunrise to sunset
Maps: Hawks Nest State Park Map & Trail Guide; USGS Fayetteville
Trail contacts: Hawks Nest State Park, 49 Hawks Nest Park Rd., Ansted 25812; (304) 658-5212; https://wvstateparks.com/park/hawks-nest-state-park

Finding the trailhead: From the New River Gorge Visitor Center just north of the New River Bridge on US 19 near Fayetteville, drive north on US 19 for 4.8 miles to the US 60 exit, Hico/Rainelle. Take

US 60 west for 7.6 miles to Hawks Nest State Park, passing through the town of Ansted. Enter the park and turn left toward the lodge. Look for the tennis courts, playground, and basketball court on your left. The GSYP Trail starts at the rear of the basketball court. GPS trailhead coordinates: 38.122002, -81.116942

The Hike

It is not often that hikers have an aerial tram to help them tackle the hardest part of their trek. But here at Hawks Nest State Park—if you time your hike correctly—there can be such an advantage. Even if you don't take the tram, the hike is not too long, but the climb out of the gorge will burn a few calories. First head from the canyon rim down to the New River on the GSYP Trail. That stands for Governors Summer Youth Program. The youth program built the trail that leads along the slopes of the gorge down to Hawks Nest Lake. You will walk many a stone step, working among boulders and stone outcrops before joining a roadbed leading to the water's edge and a boat ramp. This offers a lake's edge view.

The hike next turns up the Mill Creek embayment of Hawks Nest Lake, crossing the stream on a bridge. The tram is easily visible from here, and you can take it later. For now, explore the lakeshore, nature center, and gift shop. By the way, you can also pick up a jet boat ride up the New River. Here a large boat ascends the New River and its rapids, allowing you to experience the moving waterway deep in the heart of the gorge. As with the tram, a fee is charged. The jet boat hours run roughly in conjunction with the tram. Check ahead to make certain on the hours at www. newriverjetboats.com.

Slightly ascend along Mill Creek after picking up the Hawks Nest Rail Trail. It enters an intimate valley on a

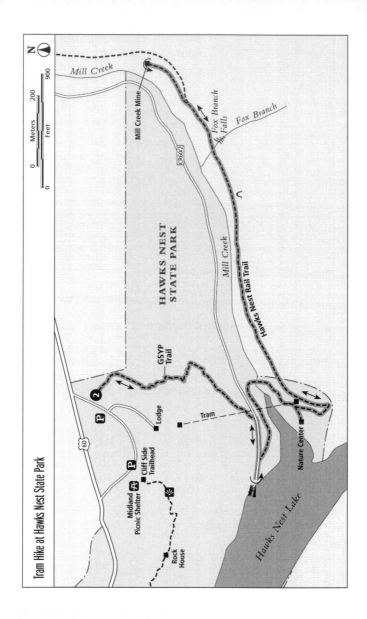

Tram Hike at Hawks Nest State Park

railroad grade. Along the way you will pass a cave with a spring emanating from it, and then view 60-foot Fox Branch Falls before turning on the side trail to reach a picnic area along Mill Creek and the site of the Mill Creek Mine, its entrance bordered in concrete. From here, walk back to the tram station and pick up the tram for an easy climb. Pay your fee at the ticket booth as you exit. Enjoy the views on the way back up!

Miles and Directions

0.0 With your back to US 60 and facing the park lodge, look left for a playground, tennis courts, and a basketball court. A natural surface foot trail, the GSYP Trail, leaves from the asphalt of the basketball court. It immediately descends along the draw and then angles its way below the park lodge. Several short switchbacks ease your descent into the gorge.

0.2 Come along a lichen-covered cliff line.

0.4 Pass under the tram line in a clearing. Reach a roadbed, turn right, and head down toward the lake.

0.5 Enjoy views from the park boat ramp. Here, gain a water's edge view of the gorge. Backtrack a short distance and then stay right along the embayment of Mill Creek to shortly span the creek on a bridge.

0.8 Pass by the tram facility, nature center, and jet boat landing. Walk toward the railroad bridge and then pick up the Hawks Nest Rail Trail. Look for mining machinery and rail tracks embedded into the soil.

1.3 Pass a cave mouth with a low-flow spring.

1.4 The trail spans Fox Branch on a trestle just above 60-foot Fox Branch Falls.

1.5 Leave left on a spur trail to the Mill Creek Mine.

1.6 Reach the mine entrance and picnic area along Mill Creek. Backtrack to the tram.

2.4 Reach the tram and take it back to the park lodge, arriving back at the trailhead.

3 Park Loop with Spur to Wolf Creek

This hike starts at the Fayetteville Town Park and then enters national park property. Travel through profuse pleasant woods on the Appalachian Plateau before dropping to meet Wolf Creek at its confluence with House Creek. An arched-span bridge crosses Wolf Creek here, adding an engineering touch to a pleasant scene where stone bluffs make for good relaxation spots. Explore nearby House Creek, where it drops in cascades to meet Wolf Creek, as well as a waterfall on Wolf Creek. Backtrack to the plateau and then make a final woodland walk, returning to Fayetteville Town Park.

Distance: 1.9-mile loop with spur
Hiking time: About 1.5 to 2.0 hours
Difficulty: Easy to moderate
Trail surface: Natural surface
Best season: Year-round
Other trail users: Bikers
Canine compatibility: Leashed dogs permitted

Fees and permits: None
Schedule: 24/7/365
Maps: Trail Areas of New River Gorge; USGS Fayetteville
Trail contacts: New River Gorge National Park and Preserve, 104 Main St., Glen Jean 25846; (304) 465-0508; www.nps.gov/neri

Finding the trailhead: From the traffic light on US 19 in Fayetteville, take Court Street, WV 16, south into downtown Fayetteville. Drive for 0.3 mile to a traffic light and Fayette Avenue. Turn left on Fayette Avenue and follow it 0.3 mile to Park Drive. Turn right on Park Drive and follow it 0.4 mile to the second entrance into Fayetteville Town Park, on your right. This second entrance is 0.1 mile past the main entrance and will be after you pass the basketball courts on your right. After turning right into the second entrance, follow the park road a short distance to a circular turnaround and trailhead parking. GPS trailhead coordinates: 38.057254, -81.091361

The Hike

Trail access is easy, and the path is used by locals for daily exercise. You can make this hike shorter and easier by simply avoiding the spur down to Wolf Creek. If you do this, elevation changes will be around 100 feet, whereas the trip down to Wolf Creek adds about another 150 feet of elevation change.

A well-maintained, singletrack path enters plateau woods of maple, sourwood, oak, and hickory. It isn't long before the loop splits. This hike heads clockwise around the loop and works into a draw. Evergreens and ferns become more prevalent. Step over a low boardwalk, leaving the draw. You will pass a shortcut leading to the Fayetteville Trail and then come to the first official intersection with the Fayetteville Trail, which leads down toward Fayette Station Road and the New River Bridge.

The spur part of this hike takes the next intersection with the Fayetteville Trail. It descends off the plateau gently, using multiple switchbacks. Mountain laurel prevails on this south-facing slope, along with greenbrier, sourwood, and sassafras. Drop deeper toward Wolf Creek on a well-graded trail. The gurgle of Wolf Creek reaches your ears as you lose elevation. Wolf Creek feeds the New River just before the New passes under the New River Bridge.

The trail reaches a pleasant locale at the confluence of House Creek and Wolf Creek. An arched bridge spans Wolf Creek, allowing good looks at the stream and its myriad rocks and bluffs. A user-created spur trail heads to House Creek. Here you can go down to the waterway and view

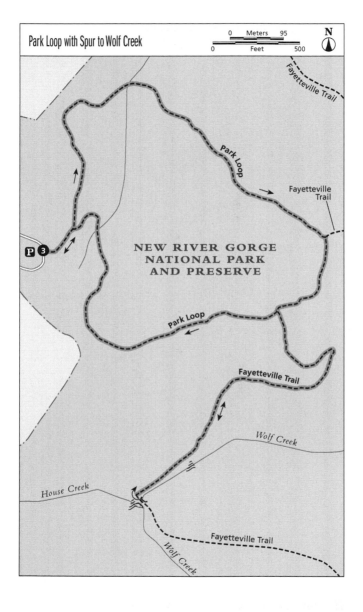

Park Loop with Spur to Wolf Creek

0 Meters 95
0 Feet 500

N

Fayetteville Trail

Park Loop

Fayetteville Trail

P 3

NEW RIVER GORGE
NATIONAL PARK
AND PRESERVE

Park Loop

Fayetteville Trail

Wolf Creek

House Creek

Fayetteville Trail

Wolf Creek

some of the several cascades that form just before House Creek flows into Wolf Creek. These waterways are best enjoyed from late winter through spring, at their historically highest flows. A rock bluff on Wolf Creek makes for a good viewing platform too.

A 0.4-mile backtrack takes you back up to the Park Loop. Continue clockwise on the circuit. The hiking is easy, and you can revel in the upland forest. A final dip into a wet-weather streambed makes but little elevation change, and then you complete the loop and the hike. Fayetteville Town Park also has asphalt trails coursing through the developed part of the park and boasts picnic shelters, restrooms, and ball fields.

Miles and Directions

0.0 Start at the circular turnaround off the second entrance into Fayetteville Town Park. A national park signboard and kiosk marks the Park Loop's beginning. Join a singletrack dirt path heading north into thick woods, away from the park's developed facilities. The Park Loop soon splits. Stay left and begin the circuit, heading clockwise.

0.2 Step over a normally dry streambed on a wooden boardwalk.

0.6 One end of the Fayetteville Trail leaves left at a signed intersection. It is 1.5 miles down to Fayette Station Road. Stay straight on the Park Loop.

0.7 This time leave the Park Loop, heading left on another segment of the Fayetteville Trail. The signpost indicates Wolf Creek is 0.4 mile distant. The Fayetteville Trail is used less than the Park Loop.

1.1 Reach the bridge over Wolf Creek, after passing an 8-foot ledge fall on Wolf Creek. To your right, House Creek meets

Wolf Creek after dropping over several small falls enshrouded among thickets of rhododendron. Backtrack.

1.5 Turn left on the Park Loop after climbing away from Wolf Creek.

1.7 The loop turns right, north. An unofficial spur from a nearby town neighborhood comes in on your left.

1.8 Bridge a wet-weather stream on a boardwalk.

1.9 Arrive back at the trailhead after meeting the other end of the loop.

4 Long Point

This very popular hike makes a mostly easy trek to a prominent rock spine culminating in a view from its tip—Long Point. From here you can see the famed New River Bridge as it crosses from one end of the New River Gorge to the other, as well as the natural features around it. But the hike is rewarding from its beginning at an easily accessible trailhead through eye-pleasing woods down to the narrow rock spine of Long Point. And elevation changes are less than 300 feet, making it easily doable by your average hiker.

Distance: 3.2-mile there-and-back
Hiking time: About 1.5 to 2.0 hours
Difficulty: Moderate
Trail surface: Crushed gravel and natural surface
Best season: Year-round
Other trail users: Bikers—trail is hikers only for last 0.2 mile

Canine compatibility: Leashed dogs permitted
Fees and permits: None
Schedule: 24/7/365
Maps: Trail Areas of New River Gorge; USGS Fayetteville
Trail contacts: New River Gorge National Park and Preserve, 104 Main St., Glen Jean 25846; (304) 465-0508; www.nps.gov/neri

Finding the trailhead: From the traffic light on US 19 in Fayetteville, take Court Street, WV 16, south for 0.7 mile to Gatewood Road (you will see a park service sign for Cunard here). Turn left on Gatewood Road and follow it for 1.8 miles to Newton Road. Turn left on Newton Road and follow it just a short distance to the trailhead on your left. GPS trailhead coordinates: 38.041717, -81.078150

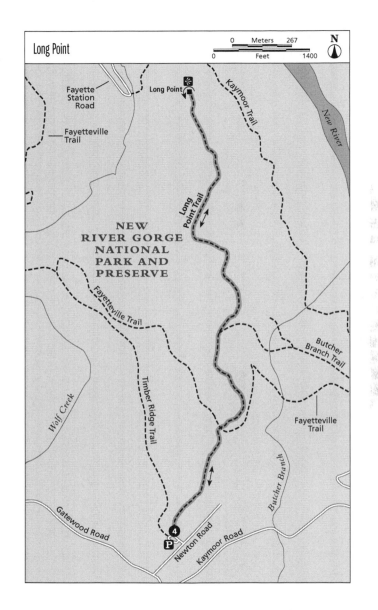

The Hike

The New River Bridge on US 19 just north of Fayetteville is the largest arch span in the Western Hemisphere. Funny thing, after you have been to Long Point, you can easily spot it while driving northbound on the bridge. Your hike to the look-off will enhance your appreciation of the New River Gorge and the bridge that spans it. This is one of the most famed bridges in the United States. The span has spawned something called Bridge Day, held on the third Saturday in October every year. Bridge Day, when the bridge is closed to through traffic, started out as a way for area residents and visitors alike to walk the bridge while soaking in the autumn splendor of the gorge. During that first year, 1985, five parachutists jumped off the bridge, creating more than a literal splash, and Bridge Day morphed into the world's largest BASE jumping event (jumping from a fixed point using a parachute, versus skydiving from a plane; BASE is an acronym for "buildings, antennas, spans, and earth").

Now over 200,000 people annually come to this extravaganza that also includes rappelers lowering themselves from the bridge, but not bungee jumpers. Bungee jumping from this bridge has become the stuff of urban legend. The bridge was started in 1974 and finished in 1977. It rises 876 feet above the New River, is 3,030 feet long, and weighs 88 million pounds. That is a whole lotta bridge to suspend!

You gain a first-rate view of the bridge from Long Point. And the hike is rewarding along the way. The path immediately enters forest but has to sneak behind some houses on Newton Road, going in and out of woodland and atop a set of three boardwalks over wetlands. Once beyond the houses, the path heads north in upland forest of hickory, oak, locust, and maple. Preserved hemlocks add an evergreen touch to the modestly undulating trail as you follow an ever-narrowing ridge.

Toward the end, the trail begins making its descent. The land peninsula becomes rockier, even more slender, and irregular. The path tunnels through dense rhododendron on a rooty track. Finally, the trail is on almost pure rock—a rock bridge if you will—with scattered chestnut oaks, pines, and blueberry bushes. Views open east toward the New River and west into Wolf Creek. Exquisite panoramas open ahead too, centered by a view down the New River Gorge with the bridge front and center. This vista is likely very crowded on Bridge Day but is worth a visit the other 364 days of the year too. And you may even have it to yourself during off times, as I have.

Miles and Directions

0.0 Leave the large parking area and join the Long Point Trail entering forest. You will soon cross the first of three short boardwalks as the trail snakes behind some nearby residences. The Timber Ridge Trail leaves from the same parking area.

0.3 Reenter full-blown woods after passing through meadows behind a set of houses on Newton Road. An elevated platform overlooks the biodiverse meadows.

0.4 Intersect the Fayetteville Trail. It leads left toward Wolf Creek and the Fayetteville Town Park and right toward Kaymoor Mine. Keep straight with the Long Point Trail.

0.7 Intersect the Butcher Branch Trail. It leaves right toward the Kaymoor Miners Trail and also has a spur leading to climbing areas. Continue straight with the Long Point Trail.

1.0 The Long Point Trail turns sharply right. The ridgeline begins falling away on both sides.

1.4 Make a decidedly steep drop amid preserved hemlocks. The trail is hikers only beyond here.

1.6 Emerge at the tip of Long Point. Absorb astounding views in three directions, highlighted with the bridge and the depth of the gorge. Backtrack.

3.2 Arrive back at the trailhead, completing the hike.

5 Kaymoor Mine Loop

What a rewarding and historic hike! Start by taking the steep Kaymoor Miners Trail and descend through alluring forest and impressive geology to reach the Kaymoor Mine, one of the most intact mine sites around. See building relics, signage, structures, and the mine itself. An optional spur takes you to the bottom of the gorge to view more history. Otherwise, the hike travels along the mid-slope of the gorge easterly in more national park–level scenery, including waterfalls, and then returns via the Craig Branch Trail, where you enjoy upland hardwoods on a doubletrack path before passing through a set of mountain-biking trails. Reach the mountain-biking trail parking area, and then it is but a short road walk to complete the loop.

Distance: 4.7-mile loop
Hiking time: About 2.5 to 3.0 hours
Difficulty: More challenging due to distance and elevation change
Trail surface: Natural surface
Best season: Year-round
Other trail users: Bikers
Canine compatibility: Leashed dogs permitted

Fees and permits: None
Schedule: 24/7/365
Maps: Trail Areas of New River Gorge; USGS Fayetteville
Trail contacts: New River Gorge National Park and Preserve, 104 Main St., Glen Jean 25846; (304) 465-0508; www.nps.gov/neri

Finding the trailhead: From US 19 in Fayetteville at a traffic light, take Court Street, WV 16, south for 0.7 mile to Gatewood Road (you will see a park service sign for Cunard here). Turn left on Gatewood Road and follow it for 1.9 miles to Kaymoor Road. Turn left on Kaymoor Road and follow it 0.9 mile to a T intersection. Turn left and

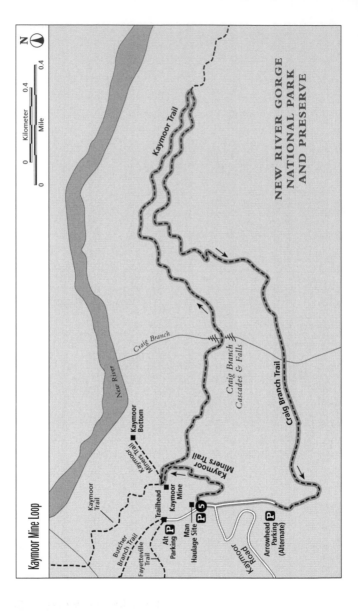

Kaymoor Mine Loop

NEW RIVER GORGE
NATIONAL PARK
AND PRESERVE

Kaymoor Trail

Craig Branch

Craig Branch
Cascades & Falls

Craig Branch Trail

New River

Kaymoor Trail

Kaymoor
Bottom

Miners Trail

Kaymoor
Trail

Butcher
Branch Trail

Fayetteville
Trail

Alt
Parking

Trailhead

Kaymoor Mine

Kaymoor
Miners Trail

Man
Haulage Site

P 5

Kaymoor
Road

Arrowhead
Parking
(Alternate)

N

Kilometer   0   0.4

Mile   0   0.4

drive a short distance to the official parking area. On foot backtrack a short distance to reach the Kaymoor Miners Trail and begin the hike there. GPS trailhead coordinates: 38.045257, -81.067653

The Hike

This is a rewarding hike for its natural beauty and New River Gorge history. Take a minute to enjoy the view from the man haulage platform near the trailhead parking area. The man haulage was an old conveyor that took people and supplies from here to the mine and on to the gorge bottom. At the Kaymoor Miners Trail, read the interpretive information before you set off downhill. Cut through a break in the cliff line. Rhododendron, beech, maple, and trailside hemlock cheer you on. Step after step after step moderates the challenging descent. Take your time on the steepest parts of the path, especially if conditions are wet.

Your thighs will be burning from keeping the brakes on by the time you reach the Kaymoor Mine. An old metal sign states, "Your family wants you to work safely." Scads of interpretive information about the mine operation and the miners themselves gives life to the artifacts from the mine. The narrow, flat mine car sheds light inside a 36-inch-high mine seam. Visit the stone buildings and other structures. The natural beauty is visible too—it is a clear shot across the gorge at the tan cliff line known as the Endless Wall. The stone outcrop is popular with rock climbers and also offers first-rate vistas into the gorge and back across at this mine.

If you are feeling frisky, take the 821 steps down to the community of Kaymoor Bottom. The recommended but challenging detour leads to more mine relics, as well as remnants of a miner community that was once down there. Of course, it is 821 steps back up. This circuit leaves the mine site and travels easterly along the mid-slope of the New River Gorge. Other mining relics are stretched along this part of the trail. Look also for grown-over debris piles and faint spurs emanating from the main path. The path remains more level than not under the tulip trees and astride big boulders. Cataracts will be heard and seen at the crossing of Craig Branch. The spillers upstream of the trail are easier to access.

During summer you may hear rafters yelling below as they crash through the whitewater. Your easy mid-slope walk becomes a little more difficult after you join the Craig Branch Trail. It is also a doubletrack path working uphill among hills and shallow vales. Partial gorge views continue. On your way up, the path winds through a field of massive boulders that enhance the geological component of the trek. Look also for scattered overhangs and ledges.

The ascent eases after reaching the top of the Appalachian Plateau. Ahead, cross the headwaters of Craig Branch. From here on the hiking is easy as you cross a couple of mountain bike trails that are part of the greater Arrowhead mountain bike trail system. The Craig Branch Trail ends at the Arrowhead parking area. From here it is a short and easy walk back to the trailhead near the Kaymoor Miners Trail.

Miles and Directions

0.0 From the parking area backtrack on the road access, and then join the Kaymoor Miners Trail. Begin a slow but steep descent on a singletrack footpath.

0.1 Leave left from an old roadbed you have been following.

0.3 Make a pair of quick switchbacks, passing under a low-flow cascade sheeting over a flat rock face. The trail remains steep. Use stone and wood steps on declivitous segments.

0.4 Reach the mine site. Explore the old mine cars, look in the mine shaft, check out the buildings, and walk west down the Kaymoor Trail to see more relics before heading east on the Kaymoor Trail to continue the loop.

1.1 Cross Craig Branch and reach the 15-foot Craig Branch Cascades and 25-foot Craig Branch Falls, which tumble above the trail, while a more difficult to access cataract spills below the trail.

1.6 Come to a view of a river rapid on a steep point.

2.1 The trail is pinched in by a gigantic boulder.

2.2 Intersect the Craig Branch Trail. Turn acutely right and head uphill, now westbound.

3.0 Bisect an incredible boulder field.

3.2 Level off atop the Appalachian Plateau.

3.7 Cross upper Craig Branch. Ahead, pass a set of mountain bike trails.

4.4 Pass around a pole gate at the Arrowhead trailhead. Turn right here and follow the gravel road toward the Kaymoor Miners Trail.

4.7 Finish the loop, arriving back at the trailhead.

6 **Diamond Point via the Endless Wall**

The rewards of this hike far outstrip the effort needed to undertake it. The highlight reel first explores a dark, brooding tributary of the New River, Fern Creek, where preserved hemlocks form the backdrop of a nearly lost fairyland forest. After bridging Fern Creek, the hike aims for the rim of the New River Gorge and the bluffs of the Endless Wall. Cruise the edge of the canyon and then take a spur trail to Diamond Point, which boasts one of the best vistas in the entire New River Gorge National Park and Preserve. Elevation changes are less than 100 feet.

Distance: 2.0-mile there-and-back
Hiking time: About 1.5 to 2.0 hours
Difficulty: Easy to moderate
Trail surface: Natural surface
Best season: Anytime when skies are clear
Other trail users: None
Canine compatibility: Leashed dogs permitted

Fees and permits: None
Schedule: 24/7/365
Maps: Trail Areas of New River Gorge; USGS Fayetteville
Trail contacts: New River Gorge National Park and Preserve, 104 Main St., Glen Jean 25846; (304) 465-0508; www.nps.gov/ neri

Finding the trailhead: From the national park visitor center on US 19 just north of the New River Bridge near Fayetteville, continue north on US 19 for 0.3 mile to Lansing-Edmond Road, CR 5/82. Turn right on Lansing-Edmond Road and follow it 1.3 miles to the Fern Creek trailhead on your right. This trailhead is at the bottom of a hill and is easy to miss. Be apprised that the eastern end of the Endless Wall

Trail is 0.5 mile distant on Lansing-Edmond Road from this trailhead. GPS trailhead coordinates: 38.063033, -81.056733

The Hike

The Endless Wall is a significant rock bluff high atop the New River Gorge that seems to go on forever. Diamond Point extends from the Endless Wall into the New River Gorge. From this rocky perch you can view many highlights of the gorge, including the New River Bridge, the preserved Kaymoor Mine, the continuation of the Endless Wall, and several heart-stopping whitewater rapids deep in the canyon below. If you are lucky, rafters will be plying the whitewater below while you are perched on Diamond Point. Hikers like us will not be the only ones appreciating this area. Climbers take advantage of the vertical bluffs of the Endless Wall and use it to scale the stony heights hundreds of feet above the New River.

But you don't have to cruise through some drab forest just to get to this viewpoint. The Fern Creek Valley is a hemlock haven and one of the places within the boundaries of the New River Gorge National Park and Preserve where park personnel have decided to preserve a large number of this evergreen. The hemlock woolly adelgid has devastated hemlocks throughout the eastern United States, and hemlock-dominated forests are now few in number. But here you can still enjoy this unusual woodland. However, it isn't just hemlocks—beech and black birch trees also favor this moist streamside environment, as does rhododendron. Fern Creek winds its way through a high-elevation valley, leaving small sandbars where it turns. The small stream has the color of tea, from tannins in the water where vegetation has decayed.

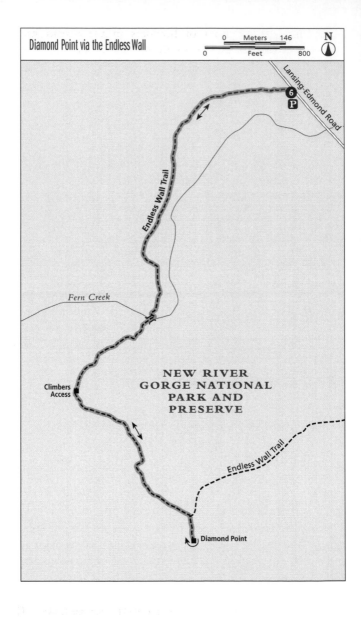

Diamond Point via the Endless Wall

0 Meters 146
0 Feet 800
N

Lansing-Edmond Road

6 P

Endless Wall Trail

Fern Creek

Climbers
Access

NEW RIVER
GORGE NATIONAL
PARK AND
PRESERVE

Endless Wall Trail

Diamond Point

Admire the plethora of boulders in the stream itself as you cross it on a wooden footbridge. Rock and water conspire to create the beauty of the New River Gorge and its tributaries. The trail climbs away from Fern Creek on a now-narrower track. You soon come alongside the rim of the gorge, now in drier-situation vegetation—sassafras, pine, and sourwood. Walk by a climber's access path. The slender trail saddles alongside the rim. User-created spurs head to sandstone edges, created by those not willing to wait for the vistas of Diamond Point. Finally, a signed spur leads right to Diamond Point. It is clearly the best view, er, views, of them all.

Several outcrops provide multiple vistas. The farthest right extends downcanyon, where part of the New River Bridge and Long Point can be seen. Ahead, you can look across the canyon at the restored Kaymoor Mine, its buildings, signs, and more. Another view opens upriver at the continuation of the Endless Wall and the curves of the gorge in the distance. The railroad lines are visible along the New. A series of rapids falls below. They are all Class III and above—Keeneys Rapids, Dudleys Dip Rapids, Double Z Rapids, and Greyhound Rapids. Wow! Take your time and check out all the panoramas. The name Diamond Point truly reflects its value. The Endless Wall Trail continues for 1.4 miles beyond the spur to Diamond Point, should you desire to extend your hike. You could then return to the Fern Creek trailhead with a half-mile road walk. Otherwise, turn around and backtrack to the trailhead from whence you came.

Miles and Directions

0.0 Leave the Lansing-Edmond Road westerly trailhead of the Endless Wall Trail. Begin heading south in a cool, lush valley of Fern Creek. Preserved hemlocks rise tall in this vale and set an evergreen tone, complemented by holly, ferns, mosses, and scads of rhododendron.

0.3 Come alongside Fern Creek. Note its tannic water.

0.5 Cross Fern Creek on a footbridge. The path narrows.

0.6 Reach the edge of the New River Gorge. The trail turns south-easterly along the edge. The New River roars hundreds of feet below.

0.7 A signed spur trail leads right to a climber's access. Keep straight on the Endless Wall Trail.

1.0 Take the short spur leading right to Diamond Point. It presents multiple rock outcrops from which to view the New River Gorge. Backtrack.

2.0 Arrive back at the trailhead, completing the hike.

7 Historic Nuttallburg Hike

The Nuttallburg area is a historic hiking destination at New River Gorge National Park and Preserve. This abandoned mine and village was given to the park service by the Nuttallburg family in 1998. By 2011 the area had been restored by the park service, including mining facilities as well as homesites. Today a series of interconnected trails makes a visit to Nuttallburg one of the best interpretive experiences in the New River Gorge. This casual stroll will take you by the coal tipple, coal conveyor, miner housing, church, and even an old school. Be prepared to learn a lot while you're on this mentally and physically stimulating hike.

Distance: 1.7-mile loop with spurs
Hiking time: About 1.5 to 3.0 hours
Difficulty: Easy
Trail surface: Gravel and natural surface
Best season: Year-round
Other trail users: None
Canine compatibility: Leashed dogs permitted

Fees and permits: None
Schedule: 24/7/365
Maps: Trail Areas of New River Gorge; USGS Fayetteville
Trail contacts: New River Gorge National Park and Preserve, 104 Main St., Glen Jean 25846; (304) 465-0508; www.nps.gov/neri

Finding the trailhead: From the national park visitor center on US 19 just north of the New River Bridge near Fayetteville, continue north on US 19 for 0.3 mile to Lansing-Edmond Road, CR 5/82. Turn right on Lansing-Edmond Road and follow it 6 miles to a T intersection in the community of Winona. Turn right here on Keeneys Creek Road, CR

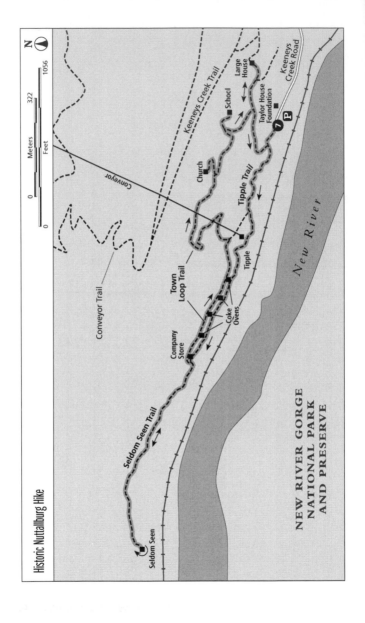

Historic Nuttallburg Hike

NEW RIVER GORGE NATIONAL PARK AND PRESERVE

New River

Seldom Seen Trail

Seldom Seen

Conveyor Trail

Company Store

Town Loop Trail

Coke Ovens

Tipple

Conveyor

Church

Keeneys Creek Trail

School

Large House

Taylor House Foundation

Tipple Trail

Keeneys Creek Road

P

7

N

Meters
0   322
Feet
0   1056

85/2. Follow Keeneys Creek Road to dead-end at Nuttallburg at 4.1 miles. GPS trailhead coordinates: 38.050116, -81.040171

The Hike

This is one of the most rewarding hikes in the New River Gorge. It took several years to restore Nuttallburg and add the trails and interpretive information. And now you can enjoy the fruits of this labor. I urge you to take your time and really soak in the natural setting and the historic overlay, and use your imagination to re-create life in this village that was a thriving coal town from the 1870s to the 1950s.

The New River, the surrounding gorge, and railroad tracks compose the setting. Interpretive information enhanced with photographs has been placed at strategic positions throughout the hike and really brings Nuttallburg to life. The coal tipple and coke ovens as well as Henry Ford's coal conveyor stand out. Ford of automobile fame was actually an owner of the mine for a period. Then you'll see the foundations of the company store. Imagine how this retailer would've been a hub of the community. Houses were scattered all around the mine area, and the hike takes you to a spot known as Seldom Seen, a "suburb" of Nuttallburg. Homesites and relics of metal and glass can be found here. Make sure and leave them for others to discover.

After backtracking from Seldom Seen, again pass the company store and coke ovens. Operating these coal-refining ovens was a hot and smoky endeavor. Life as a coal miner wasn't easy. Pass under the coal conveyor. This curved structure took coal from the mine, located upslope on the gorge, and then brought it down to the tipple and processing area, near the railroad. These mining towns couldn't have come to be without the railroad coming through the gorge—the terrain was simply too rough to move the coal otherwise. When imagining Nuttallburg, take the trees away. It wasn't the thick junglesque forest we have today. The terrain was open, and the coal conveyor stood tall and proud as it curved its way up the slope. But the river continues to roar the same as it did in Nuttallburg's day.

The Town Loop Trail leads from the level tipple area and up the mountain slope, where many of the miners lived. More relics can be seen, from old shoe soles to teacups. Pass more home foundations. You will then reach the white church, where the white townsfolk worshipped God. Even though they worked hand in hand in the mines, miners were segregated aboveground in Nuttallburg, from the schools to the churches to resident locales. Consider that as you follow the trail to a school site. Imagine all the distractions kids faced here—loud coal operation nearby, the roar of the river, and the lure of the nearby woods and water. Finally, view the stone foundation of a large house. After backtracking from there, you will complete the loop. Take note of more interpretive information in the area, including on the road to Nuttallburg, absorbing the atmosphere of this fascinating piece of the past.

Miles and Directions

0.0 Leave the parking area on a road. (The physically disabled may drive a car on this road; others must walk.) It immediately splits; stay left here. The other way is your return route. Shortly come to another split and head left on the Tipple Trail, passing under the coal tipple. Inspect the metal structure and imagine what a noisy, dusty place it would've been when the mine was active.

0.4 Intersect the Seldom Seen Trail near the foundations of the company store. Join this lesser-used path, passing by boulders and coming to a set of homesites with relics from jars to pottery to glass and metal tubs.

0.6 The trail peters out among homesites. Explore, and then backtrack to the company store.

0.8 Stay left at the company store on the Town Loop Trail, and cruise along the north side of the coke ovens.

1.0 Return to the coal tipple and conveyor. Note the other machinery and metal relics around. This area is well preserved, since it was in operation until 1958. Enjoy the view at the long, curved conveyor. Turn left, staying with the Town Loop Trail. Note all the coal beneath the conveyor.

1.2 Follow the spur trail to the town church. Backtrack, and then resume the loop.

1.4 Take the spur to the school. The sloped terrain kept everyone in shape. Backtrack.

1.5 Turn left on the Keeneys Creek Rail Trail Connector. Head up this path a short way and then overlook the frame of a large house, where one of the wealthier residents lived. The house is unremarkable in size by today's standards. Backtrack.

1.7 Arrive back at the trailhead after completing the loop.

8 Brooklyn Mine Trail

This solitude-filled hike traces the upper slope of the New River Gorge en route to the historic Brooklyn Mine. First walk an old roadbed up a hollow and then through field turning to forest. This is a favorable place to view wildlife. The mostly level walk turns into the main gorge, where you can soak in occasional views of the wooded canyon stretching to the yon. After a couple of miles, reach the Brooklyn Mine. Here the barred-over shaft and mine machinery can be viewed.

Distance: 4.0-mile there-and-back
Hiking time: About 2.0 to 2.5 hours
Difficulty: Moderate
Trail surface: Natural surface
Best season: Late fall through early spring for best views
Other trail users: Bikers, equestrians
Canine compatibility: Leashed dogs permitted

Fees and permits: None
Schedule: 24/7/365
Maps: Trail Areas of New River Gorge; USGS Fayetteville, Thurmond
Trail contacts: New River Gorge National Park and Preserve, 104 Main St., Glen Jean 25846; (304) 465-0508; www.nps.gov/neri

Finding the trailhead: From US 19 in Oak Hill, take the East Main Street exit. Join WV 16 north and follow it 0.5 mile to Gatewood Road. Turn right on Gatewood Road, WV 14 (look for the national park sign indicating Cunard), and follow it for 5.5 miles. Turn right on Cunard Road, CR 9, and follow it 1.7 miles, just past the Cunard Baptist Church, and then turn left at the park access road for Cunard. The access road immediately turns left again. Stay with the access road for 0.4 mile to the trailhead on your right. The parking area is just past the trailhead on your right. GPS trailhead coordinates: 38.000667, -81.033250

The Hike

This hike travels a ridgeline dividing appropriately named Coal Run from the New River. This whole area was heavily mined over several decades, and mining evidence can easily be seen today. Coal Run drops in a scenic 35-foot sheet waterfall just north of the trailhead. You will hear it from the parking area and can view the drop from the access road. Be careful, however, as commercial rafting buses travel this road to begin running rapids on the New River access below. The hike begins on a foot-friendly, doubletrack path heading up a hollow. It quickly turns and levels off in an area reforesting from being strip-mined. Note the shallow ponds left over and also the steep hillside with a few barren spots. This occurred much later than the deep pit mine you are hiking to visit.

The Brooklyn Mine was opened in the 1890s. It was operated by several companies and finally closed down in the 1950s. The mine stands 800 feet above the river and the railroad that hauled the coal. A tipple was located at the railroad and connected to the mine site by an 1,800-foot-long conveyor. Mine cars filled with coal were sent down to the tipple and railroad and then brought back up empty using steam power. The Brooklyn operation at the river bottom had its own electrical power plant generating the steam. There were also coke ovens down there converting the coal to coke, a distilled, energy-rich by-product of coal used in industry. A community of workers was scattered around the Brooklyn operation.

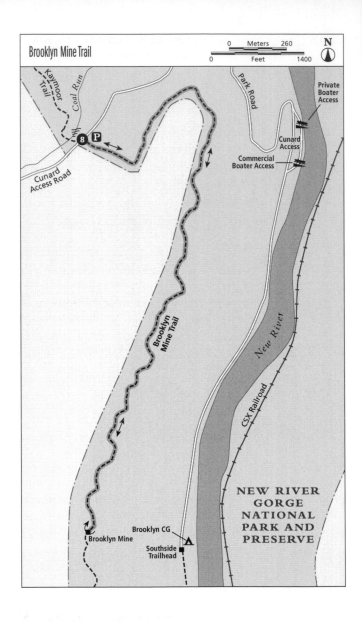

The trail is one of the few park trails open to equestrians, but as a practical matter they are hardly seen on the path. Maple, oak, black birch, and tulip trees shade the track. Autumn olive, a nonnative plant with fruits that attract wildlife in late fall and winter, has been planted as well. After you turn into the New River Gorge, the sky opens to your left. In winter you will be able to see clearly into the gorge and beyond. The scene can be quite dramatic when clouds are swirling in the valley below. The roar of the New River rises up the chasm.

The trail begins a pattern of rising just a bit along rib ridges, then dipping into hollows, then rising around a rib ridge, and so on, keeping south toward the Brooklyn Mine. Sporadic views open even in summer, but when the leaves are off, the panoramas will be stunning. You're almost there upon reaching a horse hitching post. This is one of the wider spots in the trail. Continue forward and you soon come upon the mine shaft, to the right of the trail. It is barred, but you can still look inside to see the wooden beams and metal artifacts of this low entrance. To your left you will see part of the incline that took the coal to the bottom of the gorge. These unstable mine remnants are fenced off, so please respect the closure. The trail continues for 0.7 mile beyond this mine shaft and then dead-ends.

Miles and Directions

0.0 Pick up the Brooklyn Mine Trail and leave the Cunard access road, heading uphill on a doubletrack path away from Coal Run.

0.2 Level out in a partly forested flat. Begin hiking past forested strip mines. Berry vines grow in thick ranks during summer.

0.4 Walk near small ponds. Look for cliffs in the woods to your right.

0.5 Turn south into the New River Gorge. The land drops 800 feet below.

1.1 Pass a grove of white pines.

1.9 Come upon a horse hitching post.

2.0 Reach the shaft of the Brooklyn Mine. To your left are ruins of the coal conveyor and other mine buildings. Please do not go around the fence dividing this from the trail. Backtrack.

4.0 Arrive back at the trailhead, completing the hike.

9 Red Ash via Southside Trail

This hike traces the old Chesapeake & Ohio Railroad from the abandoned mining town of Brooklyn along a scenic stretch of the New River to end at the also-abandoned mining town of Red Ash. You can see relics of Red Ash, the site of a 1900 mining disaster that killed forty-six men. Mother Nature's hand has restored the area to its natural splendor, and you can revel in the tall trees rising on bluff-pocked hillsides as well as the roaring rapids of the New River.

Distance: 3.6-mile there-and-back

Hiking time: About 2.0 to 2.5 hours

Difficulty: Easy to moderate

Trail surface: Natural surface

Best season: Year-round

Other trail users: Bikers

Canine compatibility: Leashed dogs permitted

Fees and permits: None

Schedule: 24/7/365

Maps: Trail Areas of New River Gorge; USGS Thurmond

Trail contacts: New River Gorge National Park and Preserve, 104 Main St., Glen Jean 25846; (304) 465-0508; www.nps.gov/neri

Finding the trailhead: From US 19 in Oak Hill, take the East Main Street exit. Join WV 16 north and follow it 0.5 mile to Gatewood Road. Turn right on Gatewood Road, WV 14 (look for the national park sign indicating Cunard), and follow it for 5.5 miles. Turn right on Cunard Road, CR 9, and follow it 1.7 miles, just past the Cunard Baptist Church, and then turn left at the park access road for Cunard. The access road immediately turns left again. Stay with the access road to reach the New River. Once down here, stay right and pass through the commercial boat access area, and then join a gravel road at the far end of the commercial river access parking. Follow this gravel road 1 mile to dead-end at the trailhead. GPS trailhead coordinates: 37.983917, -81.028133

The Hike

The hike begins at what was once Brooklyn, a New River mining town. Today there is a small camping area at the trailhead. Look for evidence of the processing of coal from the Brooklyn Mine hundreds of feet above. There is also loose coal around the parking area. This hike leaves Brooklyn and heads upstream along the New River, tracing the old Chesapeake & Ohio Railroad bed. Along the way you will pass river accesses to beaches, boulders, and rapids. The elevated trail presents exhilarating views of the river and the other side of the gorge rising in the distance. Elevation changes are insignificant. The easy walking allows you to appreciate the inexorable hardwood forest of beech, tulip, maple, and oak, and a whole lot of buckeye. Bluffs rise on your right as you travel up the path.

The trail leads to Surprise Rapid, a Class III drop. It comes just after the New River makes a sharp bend. Boaters are surprised by this cataract because it comes so soon after the bend. Surprise Rapid was created by Ephraim Creek, just upstream across the river, depositing rock debris into the waterway.

As you walk ahead, the trail bisects railroad cuts before curving southwesterly with the river. Look for embedded railroad ties in the trail bed. A large flat lies below you, cut off in places by a river channel, and is known as Red Ash Island, where the Red Ash Cemetery and other relics can be seen. Reach visible concrete relics near the trail. This is the beginning of Red Ash. Explore the flats below and up the trail as well, finding concrete and brick parts of structures.

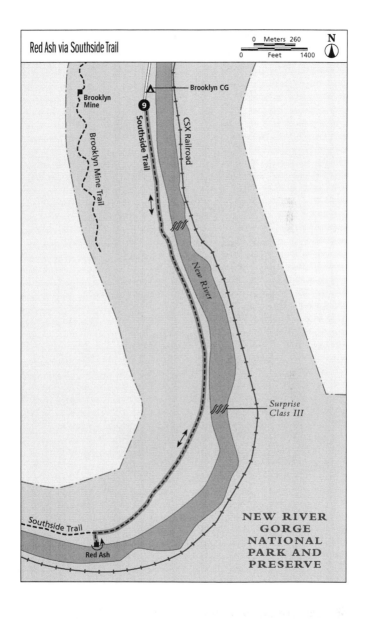

Red Ash via Southside Trail

0 — Meters — 260
0 — Feet — 1400

N

Brooklyn CG

Brooklyn Mine

Brooklyn Mine Trail

9 Southside Trail

CSX Railroad

New River

Surprise Class III

Southside Trail

Red Ash

NEW RIVER
GORGE
NATIONAL
PARK AND
PRESERVE

Communities such as Red Ash were forced to spread out along the narrow flats of the gorge bottom. A 1913 topographic map shows about thirty dwellings in the riverside flat. The Red Ash Mine was operated from 1891 until 1920, when the mine was connected to the nearby Rush Run Mine. But Red Ash was known for the horrific accident of March 6, 1900. The previous night a machine operator had improperly ventilated the mine, allowing methane gas to accumulate. The next morning employees entered the mine before it was checked for gas. Their lights set off the methane, which in turn ignited coal dust in the air, which in turn ignited kegs of blasting powder. Forty-six men died, mostly from carbon monoxide poisoning. Unfortunately, another accident occurred in 1905. Thirteen miners were killed in the mine when a mine car ran over some misplaced explosives, setting them off and igniting coal dust, which blew throughout the mine. Then a rescue party entered the mine and their flaming lights set off another explosion, killing the eleven would-be rescuers. The explosion shot flames out of the mine, blowing bystanders downhill to the river. The community of Red Ash was abandoned after the mine was closed. Most of the dwellings were dismantled. Today you can see remnants of Red Ash fading into obscurity. It is no longer marked on modern-day topographic maps.

Miles and Directions

0.0 Leave the Brooklyn camping area, passing around a pole gate. The New River flows to your left and a steep wooded hillside rises to your right.

0.2 Pass a river beach access on your left. More beach accesses are ahead.

0.5 Pass an unnamed Class II-III rapid on your left. A user-created trail leads down to the shoal.

0.7 High bluffs rise to your right among the trees.

1.0 Look for a wet-weather waterfall dripping from the cliff line to your right.

1.2 Reach Surprise Rapid on your left.

1.8 Find a concrete post to the left of the trail. This marks the beginning of Red Ash. After exploring, backtrack.

3.6 Arrive back at the trailhead, completing the hike.

10 Babcock State Park Hike

This loop is a fine sampler hike at the facility- and nature-rich state park located on a tributary of the New River, Glade Creek. First you will start at the park's fully operable gristmill and then climb away from the scenic stream and mill, ascending to the Island-in-the-Sky, a cool stone pillar rising above Glade Creek. Grab a view and then hike a bluff above Glade Creek on the Wilderness Trail. You will return to Glade Creek via the Triple Creek Trail, crossing intermittent streambeds. Walk the shores of Boley Lake just before completing the loop. Give yourself ample time to enjoy other park trails and facilities.

Distance: 3.4-mile loop
Hiking time: About 2.0 to 3.0 hours
Difficulty: Moderate
Trail surface: Natural surface
Best season: Year-round
Other trail users: Bikers
Canine compatibility: Leashed dogs permitted

Fees and permits: None
Schedule: Dawn to dusk
Maps: Babcock State Park; USGS Danese
Trail contacts: Babcock State Park, 486 Babcock Rd., Clifftop 25831; (304) 438-3004; https://wvstateparks.com/park/babcock-state-park

Finding the trailhead: From the national park visitor center on US 19 just north of the New River Bridge near Fayetteville, continue north on US 19 for 4.9 miles to US 60, Midland Trail. Take US 60 east and follow it 9.4 miles, then stay right with WV 41 south toward Clifftop. Follow WV 41 south for 3.6 miles to the main entrance to Babcock State Park. Enter the park and veer left toward the gristmill. Reach the mill and bridge at 0.4 mile. Park on the right near the ranger station or across the creek. The Island-in-the-Sky Trail is on the far side of the bridge over Glade Creek, near the gristmill. GPS trailhead coordinates: 37.979333, -80.946433

The Hike

The first part of the hike explores the geologically interesting Island-in-the-Sky. It is one of those fun trails that takes you through boulder gardens and involves a little bit of climbing but is doable by most everyone. You will circle around a pillar, under a rock overhang, and come to stone steps that take you to the rocky top. Here stands a rustic stone-and-wood shelter amid pines and blueberries. The views are limited to the immediate gorge of Glade Creek, which circles around you. The hike then drops off the pillar and to a park road. The Wilderness Trail leads away from park facilities. The Glade Creek Gorge drops away.

A mostly easy track leads to the intersection with the Triple Creek Trail. The undulating path works its way through rich forest and emerges at a parking area off Park Forest Road 801. A short road walk leads to Boley Lake. If you want to add to your mileage, simply take the Lake View Trail around the impoundment. Otherwise cross the dam. A short connector leads back to the gristmill and hike's end.

Babcock is one of West Virginia's first state parks. The Civilian Conservation Corps developed the preserve that opened July 1, 1937. In picking this locale the state didn't anticipate how well located the park would be for the future, considering the rise in popularity of rafting and hiking in what would become New River Gorge National Park and Preserve. Babcock abuts New River Gorge National Park and Preserve and is best known for the Old Mill down on Glade Creek. The reconstructed structure includes pieces of authentic mills from around the Mountain State. Meal is

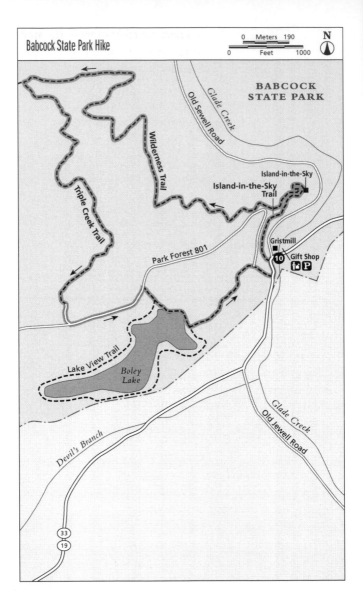

actually ground there today. There are daily tours in the summer and on weekends during the spring and fall. The park campground is also a draw. It fills just about every weekend during the summer.

Around 20 miles of hiking and mountain-biking trails wind through Babcock, in addition to the hike detailed here. The Old Sewell Road leads down to the New River, where you can check out the waters. Visitors can bike a 12-mile loop by using Old State Road and Old Sewell Road. Manns Creek Gorge Trail also offers views. There is a stable right near the campground that offers guided horseback rides and also pony rides for kids. Boley Lake features 19 acres of fishing. You can also rent paddleboats, rowboats, and canoes to explore the still waters. Game courts are on-site, and a park naturalist holds programs during the summer. Considering the above, it simply makes sense to add other activities to this hike.

Miles and Directions

0.0 Start your hike near the gristmill on the Island-in-the-Sky Trail. Take the singletrack rocky path uphill in deep woods and rhododendron. The trail soon narrows and then comes along a cliff line.

0.2 Circle around a massive rock pillar rising above you.

0.4 After dropping from the stone pillar, reach a park road and pick up the Wilderness Trail, located on the far side of the road to the right as you emerge from the woods. Climb on a wider track open to mountain bikes.

1.1 Bridge a small stream.

1.7 Intersect the Triple Creek Trail. Turn left here, descending into a series of shallow drainages divided by low hills.

2.6 Emerge from woods at the park swimming pool parking area. Take the road right, and then turn left and walk the roadside toward Boley Lake.

2.9 Leave from the road right to the Boley Lake parking area. Pick up the Lake View Trail and head left. Pass over Boley Lake Dam (or take Lake View Trail around the impoundment if you desire more miles).

3.1 Look left for a hiking trail leaving left and downhill just after crossing the dam. Descend along Camp #15 Branch in thick evergreens.

3.3 Emerge on the park road above the gristmill. Turn right.

3.4 Arrive back at the gristmill and the trailhead.

11 Rend Trail

Start your hike in the mining community of Minden. A gentle downhill leads past boulders, bluffs, and soaring woods, as well as falls aplenty in season. Pass old mile markers from when the path was a rail line. This old railroad grade once connected the mines of Minden with the New River Gorge railroad lines below. Along the way you cross multiple trestles that present scenic looks into Arbuckle Creek. The hike culminates in a cleared view of the New River and its white-water rapids near the historic town of Thurmond.

Distance: 3.6-mile there-and-back

Hiking time: About 2.0 to 2.5 hours

Difficulty: Moderate

Trail surface: Natural surface

Best season: Year-round, winter through spring for waterfalls

Other trail users: Bikers

Canine compatibility: Leashed dogs permitted

Fees and permits: None

Schedule: 24/7/365

Maps: Trail Areas of New River Gorge; USGS Thurmond

Trail contacts: New River Gorge National Park and Preserve, 104 Main St., Glen Jean 25846; (304) 465-0508; www.nps.gov/neri

Finding the trailhead: From US 19 in Oak Hill, take the East Main Street exit. Join WV 16 north and follow it just a short distance to turn left on Minden Road, WV 17. Do not turn right on Old Minden Road or Minden Avenue, which are both in immediate proximity. Follow Minden Road as it curves back under US 19, going for 2 miles to a right turn over a bridge to the trailhead. This right turn is just across from a left turn to Thurbon Road. GPS trailhead coordinates: 37.975755, -81.108915

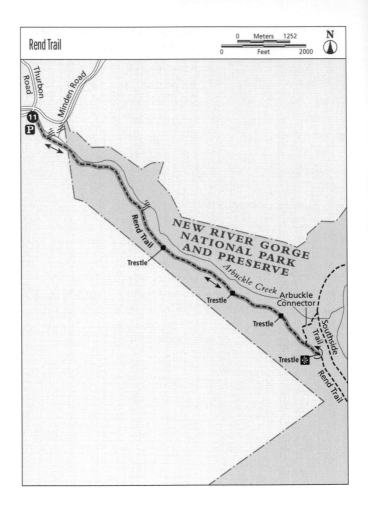

The Hike

This trail was formerly known as the Thurmond-Minden Trail, since it uses a railroad line connecting a pair of once-thriving coal communities. Minden is still heavily populated with close-knit houses and plenty of residents, whereas Thurmond was essentially abandoned and is now a showpiece of the New River Gorge National Park and Preserve historic assets, on the National Register of Historic Places. The area around the trailhead was once heavily mined. To move the coal out of the mines of Minden, the Rend Railroad was built, using the watershed of Arbuckle Creek as a connector. This enabled the coal to be taken from these upper mines down to the railroad and processing areas of Thurmond and the lines of the New River, where it was shipped to market.

Minden was originally known as Rend, named for Paddy Rend, who opened the Minden Mine in 1899. The mine was very successful, drawing in hundreds of employees whose descendants still live in some of the remaining company-built houses. Interestingly, Minden was named for a town in Germany. When the mine was purchased by Charles and Edward Berwind, they renamed it in honor of the birthplace of their mother.

The railroad line connecting Minden to Thurmond was finished in 1902 and in use until 1972. Today, instead of locomotives echoing through the valley, you hear Arbuckle Creek crashing in frequent impressive cascades and falls. Pea Ridge rises to your right as you travel down trail. A look at the Thurmond topographic map shows seams of coal around the 1,700-foot elevation near Minden. This was known as the Sewell seam and was very productive. The mine played out in the 1950s. If you drive around the community, old processing facilities are still scattered among the dwellings.

The wide trail makes for easy hiking, allowing you to absorb the scenery. Note the old whistle stop reminder. You will also see train mile markers. Soak in the rich forest down on Arbuckle Creek below. Blasted walls, created when the rail line was built, rise to your right. They are now covered with moss and vegetation in many places. Natural bluffs are bountiful as well. Resting benches are situated throughout the trail.

Ahead you will come to the first of four trestles. These restored wooden structures enhance the views. The Rend Trail continues into the widening Arbuckle Creek Valley. You'll see more evidence of the railroad, including old wooden ties, mile markers, and other relics. The roar of the New River reaches your ears. You soon meet the Arbuckle Connector, a spur trail that links this path to the Southside Trail. This hike continues beyond that trail intersection over one last trestle, reaching a cleared view of the New River near Thurmond as the watercourse curves from sight. Live railroad tracks run on river right. The confluence of Arbuckle Creek and the New River is visible in the foreground. When the leaves are off the trees, you'll also be able to clearly see Thurmond. The Rend Trail continues into the New River Valley and then turns up Dunloup Creek to reach its other trailhead after a total distance of 3.4 miles from Minden.

Miles and Directions

0.0 Leave the Minden trailhead, passing around a vehicle barrier. Arbuckle Creek flows to your left in cascades. Note the piers of an abandoned railroad bridge over Arbuckle Creek.

0.1 Pass a whistle stop reminder. The "W" on the post indicates the spot where the conductor was to pull his whistle before entering Minden.

0.4 Pass a railroad mile marker on your left. These kept engineers apprised of their position on the railroad.

0.7 Cross the first trestle. It spans a tributary of Arbuckle Creek.

1.2 Pass a bluff with an exposed coal seam. Just ahead cross a second, longer trestle. This works past a very steep unstable hillside.

1.4 A dripping spring flows under the trail from the hillside to your right. A railroad mile marker is just ahead.

1.5 Cross the third trestle. You are close enough to the New River to gain views of the big water.

1.7 The Arbuckle Connector leaves left to meet the Southside Trail.

1.8 Pass a fourth trestle and then come to an inspiring cleared view of the New River. This is a good place to turn around. Backtrack toward Minden.

3.6 Arrive back at the trailhead, completing the hike.

12 Stone Cliff Trail

Start this hike at a popular camping and boat access on the New River. Trace an old riverside road upriver. Multiple water accesses are available from the doubletrack path, including beaches, still water, and rapids. The walk is mostly easy, with only moderate ups and downs. End at a river rapid, where you can explore a rocky beach. Combine this hike with a visit to the nearby Thurmond Historic District, a coal-driven boomtown from a century back, now on the National Register of Historic Places.

Distance: 4.0-mile there-and-back
Hiking time: About 2.0 to 2.5 hours
Difficulty: Moderate
Trail surface: Natural surface
Best season: Summer for swimming and fishing
Other trail users: Bikers
Canine compatibility: Leashed dogs permitted

Fees and permits: None
Schedule: 24/7/365
Maps: Trail Areas of New River Gorge; USGS Thurmond
Trail contacts: New River Gorge National Park and Preserve, 104 Main St., Glen Jean 25846; (304) 465-0508; www.nps.gov/neri

Finding the trailhead: From US 19 near Glen Jean, between mile markers 7.5 and 8.0, north of Beckley and south of Oak Hill, look for the New River Gorge sign for Glen Jean and Thurmond. Leave US 19 for WV 16/61 north. Take WV 16/61 north for 0.5 mile, and then turn right on CR 25/9. Travel just a short distance, coming near New River Gorge park headquarters, and then turn left on Thurmond Road, CR 25. Drive 6.1 miles on CR 25, and then turn right at a three-way intersection, toward Stone Cliff. Drive for 1.4 more miles, and then stay right on a gravel road just before CR 25 crosses the New River on a bridge. Follow the gravel road past the boat launch to the picnic area. The trail starts on the upstream side of the picnic area. Note: All the above turns are signed, and finding the trail is easier than the directions imply. GPS trailhead coordinates: 37.932500, -81.063417

The Hike

While you're down here, make sure and take time to explore the nearby Thurmond Historic District. It is an old railroad town that followed the coal mining boom times in the New River Gorge. Here you can explore the old buildings and see firsthand a place left largely intact from its heyday. During the summer, the park service runs a visitor center in the old railroad depot, which still operates as an Amtrak stop.

Stone Cliff is a popular jumping-off point for commercial boating operations. Paddlers like to put in here and enjoy a relatively milder trip ending at Brooklyn. It is below Brooklyn where the biggest brawling cataracts occur in the New River Gorge. Stone Cliff also has a primitive camping area. Most of the sites are on a tan beach down by the New River. The beach is large and is used by swimmers and anglers in addition to campers. A shaded picnic area is situated at the trailhead. Restrooms and a changing area are within sight of the parking area.

Leave the developed area on the Stone Cliff Trail. River birch, black birch, beech, pawpaw, and tulip trees rise where rocks don't occupy the terrain. Buckeyes proliferate. A steep slope rises to your right. The river sings below. Soon cross Little Stony Creek, an often dry waterway draining the highland plateau above. You'll cross more streambeds ahead.

Water accesses are frequent, even when the trail is well above the New River. The most popular accesses lead to

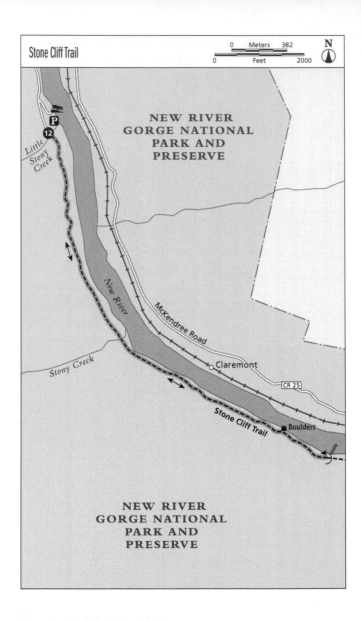

boulders, gravel bars, or rapids. The New River exhibits a big brawling nature at this point. Look across for some ruins of the community of Claremont rising above the forest. When the more than fifty coal-mining hamlets were strung out along the New, river running and rafting rapids was unheard of, though fishing was a popular pastime when miners weren't working the coal. The town of Thurmond was the wealthiest and most successful New River coal town. Several mine owners lived here. At one time Thurmond's banks held more deposits than any other institution in West Virginia.

The coal was always in the valley, but the railroad is what made it feasible to transport. And when the railroad came through, the mines followed. Thurmond boomed, then busted as less coal came out of local mines combined with the Great Depression. After that it was a long and slow decline until the railroad offices closed in 1984, the same year Thurmond was placed on the National Register of Historic Places. In 1995 the National Park Service opened the visitor center in Thurmond. That was also when the post office finally closed.

Continue to enjoy viewing the river and the other side of the gorge. In winter these panoramas will be nearly unobstructed. CR 25 and the CSX Railroad run along the far side of the river. Watch for big boulders that make ideal picnic or riverside-relaxing locales. Come to a nice rapid at 2.0 miles, with a beach and ample rocks. This is a good place to explore the river. The Stone Cliff Trail continues 0.7 mile farther if you want to extend your hike. Otherwise turn around and backtrack to your starting point.

Miles and Directions

0.0 Leave the Stone Cliff Picnic Area and work around some vehicle-blocking boulders. Join a doubletrack path heading upstream with the New River to your left.

0.1 Cross Little Stony Creek, a bouldery waterway that lives up to its name.

0.4 Reach a high point above the river. You have ascended around 100 feet. From here the trail works downhill more than not.

0.7 Return to the river's edge.

0.9 Step over boulder-laden Stony Creek. The New River is quiet hereabouts.

1.7 Come alongside a rapid. There are some tempting boulder accesses here, including one large flat boulder that makes for a good relaxation spot.

2.0 Come alongside a larger rapid with a beach. Here hikers can check out the shoal, fish, or explore the beach. Backtrack, though the trail continues for 0.7 mile more.

4.0 Arrive back at the Stone Cliff Picnic Area and trailhead.

13 Grandview Rim Trail

This is the signature hike of the Grandview area. The rewards start almost immediately after leaving the trailhead. It is but a short distance to the rim of the New River Gorge. Just a few more strides lead to the North Overlook, where you are treated to an unimpeded vista of the incredible chasm cut by the New River as it bullies through West Virginia highlands. From there the Grandview Rim Trail skirts the edge of the gorge, passing more overlooks along the canyon precipice, and through preserved hemlock forests. The Turkey Spur Overlook awaits at trail's end. Feel the natural air conditioner, a geological feature, and then climb steps to Turkey Spur Rock, with multiple vistas from its crest. Hikers are guaranteed to enjoy the return trip on this trail treasure.

Distance: 2.8-mile there-and-back
Hiking time: About 2.0 to 3.0 hours
Difficulty: Moderate
Trail surface: Natural surface
Best season: Year-round
Other trail users: None
Canine compatibility: Leashed dogs permitted

Fees and permits: None
Schedule: 24/7/365
Maps: Trail Areas of New River Gorge; USGS Prince
Trail contacts: New River Gorge National Park and Preserve, 104 Main St., Glen Jean 25846; (304) 465-0508; www.nps.gov/neri

Finding the trailhead: From exit 129 on I-64 east of Beckley, take WV 9, Grandview Road, north for 4.9 miles to the left turn toward Turkey Spur Road and the picnic shelters. Turn left here and then shortly turn right toward the North Overlook and Picnic Shelter #1. GPS trailhead coordinates: 37.833383, -81.065667

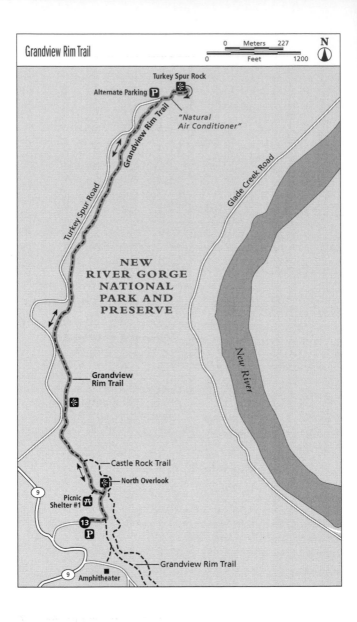

The Hike

Start the hike at a popular parking area near Picnic Shelter #1 and the short walk to the North Overlook. The remarkable view is shared by hikers and those wanting a quick and easy panorama. The sandstone bluffs open the terrain before you, allowing visitors to absorb the size and scope of this improbable canyon. Here you can look easterly up the New River Gorge for miles, until the river and its sloping massifs and deeply cut tributaries fade into the back of beyond. Nearer, the rapids and the village of Quinnimont, where the first coal was extracted from the New River Gorge, are visible downstream. The view is enough to satisfy some, but for the hiker there is more around the bend.

Rhododendron crowds the path and makes for a dusky passageway as you resume the Grandview Rim Trail. Pass a spur trail leading left to Picnic Shelter #1. Level land stretches west while the canyon drops east some 1,300 feet to the river. Oak, mountain laurel, and red maple complement the rhododendron. Hemlock is holding on well here, since the park has treated the evergreens to ward off the hemlock woolly adelgid, a nonnative invasive bug that devastated hemlocks throughout the eastern United States. Enjoy these sheltered evergreen copses, as they will be rarer and rarer as time proceeds.

Turkey Spur Road runs parallel to the Grandview Rim Trail, and they often come close together. However, this doesn't detract from the hike. In fact, hikers use the road to make one-way hikes, leaving a car at Turkey Spur Overlook, your destination. Ahead you will reach a developed overlook that presents an eye-popping view. During leaf-off the trailside views will be nearly continuous.

The trail undulations thus far have been minimal, though the path does undulate. Exposed sandstone is often covered in moss. The path becomes rocky and narrow as you come closer and closer to Turkey Spur Rock. Arrive at the north parking area, and then the highlights start coming fast and furious. Pick up the trail leading right around an immense rock outcrop. The sheer rock wall rises to your left. Enter a geological fairyland. Soon come to a wooden post marked "A." This is the natural air conditioner, a rock crevice that blows cool air on the warmest of days. Continue straight and then come to a steep set of wooden steps. This allows access to the top of the Turkey Spur Rock. Once on the crest of this stone pillar, you can go right or left. Overlooks extend in both directions. Enjoy them. It is a fitting climax to an area known as Grandview. Some hikers return via Turkey Spur Road, but I believe the trail is best. You will certainly pick up details you missed on the way out, when the grand overlooks hold sway over nature's more minute features.

Miles and Directions

0.0 From the east side of the parking area, with Picnic Shelter #1 to your left, take the wide trail heading east toward North Overlook. Quickly reach a trail intersection and head left on the Grandview Rim Trail. After a few hundred feet a spur leads right through rhododendron and opens to the North Overlook. Backtrack a short distance, resuming northbound on the Grandview Rim Trail.

0.3 Dip to a trail intersection. Here the narrow Castle Rock Trail comes in from your right. Keep straight on the Grandview Rim Trail. Continue tunneling through rhododendron.

0.4 Come very near Turkey Spur Road for the first time. Ahead reach another developed overlook. This one has an even better upstream vista. The trail stays along the rim in sourwoods and pines, alternating with cool rhododendron tunnels.

0.8 Walk through an extensive hemlock copse.

1.1 Descend by wood and earth steps to a gap where you come near Turkey Spur Road once again. Step over a drainage on a little wooden bridge. Slip over to the river side of the ridge.

1.3 Emerge at the Turkey Spur trailhead parking area. Stay right on the hiking trail. Shortly pass the natural air conditioner, blowing cool air between giant boulders. Next ascend wooden stairs to the top of a stone pillar.

1.4 Enjoy multiple overlooks from atop the pillar. Absorb the views of the gorge and then backtrack.

2.8 Arrive back at the trailhead and the North Overlook parking area.

14 Castle Rock Loop

This is arguably the most fascinating 1.2 miles of trailway at New River Gorge. Start near the Grandview Visitor Center (they don't call it Grandview for nothin'!) and stroll out to the Main Overlook. It provides a breathtaking panorama of the canyon below. From there, join the rocky and challenging Castle Rock Trail, working your way along the base of a dramatic cliff line in a geological wonderland, with boulders, bluffs, and overhangs. Climb back to the rim, and then pass more developed overlooks, each illustrating the case for preserving this special slice of the Mountain State. Be apprised that though the hike is short, the Castle Rock Trail is challenging, with irregular footing.

Distance: 1.2-mile loop
Hiking time: About 1.0 to 2.0 hours
Difficulty: Moderate
Trail surface: Natural surface
Best season: Year-round
Other trail users: None
Canine compatibility: Leashed dogs permitted

Fees and permits: None
Schedule: 24/7/365
Maps: Trail Areas of New River Gorge; USGS Prince
Trail contacts: New River Gorge National Park and Preserve, 104 Main St., Glen Jean 25846; (304) 465-0508; www.nps.gov/neri

Finding the trailhead: From exit 129 on I-64 east of Beckley, take WV 9 north, Grandview Road, for 4.9 miles, then turn right toward the Grandview Visitor Center and Main Overlook. Curve three-quarters of the way around the loop road circling the Grandview Visitor Center and then park near the sign indicating Main Overlook. GPS trailhead coordinates: 37.830527, -81.062990

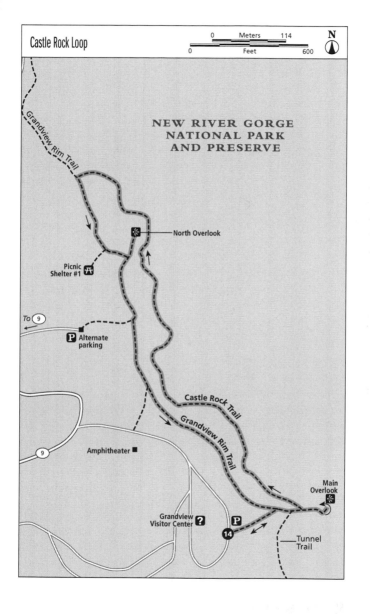

Castle Rock Loop

New River Gorge National Park and Preserve

North Overlook

Picnic Shelter #1

To 9

Alternate parking

Castle Rock Trail

Grandview Rim Trail

Grandview Rim Trail

Amphitheater

9

Grandview Visitor Center

14

Main Overlook

Tunnel Trail

N

Meters 114

Feet 600

The Hike

Make sure and stop in the visitor center if it is open. The New River Gorge is rich in human and natural history. You can enjoy informative displays within. An accessible stone walkway leads through a park-like setting before making the edge of the gorge and a sandstone outcrop, the Main Overlook. Below, white river rapids contrast with darker moving waters. The CSX Railroad mimics the river bends. Wooded canyon walls rise at angles from the New River. The curves of the gorge turn upstream and down, divided by Backus Mountain, eventually bending completely from sight. The enormity of the gorge is awe inspiring. What a start to a hike!

The Castle Rock Trail is completely dissimilar to the walkway leading to the Main Overlook. The uneven, stony track snakes between rhododendron, ferns, and mosses. Trees grab purchase where they can on the jagged slope. Take your time and the footing will not be a problem. In places natural stones have been laid to create steps that moderate the path. It isn't long before you sidle alongside a rising sheer cliff line. Hemlock, red maple, and black birch form a green backdrop to the tan-colored bluffs. Fallen boulders and rocks litter the floor below the cliffs. You walk among them. Parts of the trail travel under overhangs, keeping the hiking dry despite any precipitation. Make sure to look upon these bluffs, noting small trees, ferns, and other vegetation clinging to crevices.

The bluffs become larger as you progress, rising upwards of 100 feet. The rock colors stretch across the rainbow—auburn, gray, charcoal, rust, and brown. Look also for seams of exposed coal. Though this area was not mined, it gives you an idea of this valuable mineral's presence in the New River Gorge. Watch for sporadic undeveloped overlooks into the waters below. Pass one last cliff line and then ascend stone steps to meet the Grandview Rim Trail.

The walking becomes much easier on this wide, level, and well-used path. You can stop for a bite to eat at Picnic Shelter #1. The shelter has a fireplace in it, and there are also picnic tables stretched out over a grassy and shaded lawn. Most hikers will push on to the North Overlook, which rivals the Main Overlook in scenic value. More developed overlooks lie ahead, as does a side trail to the North Overlook parking area. Continue south along Grandview Rim Trail back to where you started. Upon completing the loop portion of the hike, I bet you will walk out to the Main Overlook to soak in one more panorama of this American treasure.

Miles and Directions

- **0.0** As you look out from the visitor center front entrance, take the stone slab trail eastbound toward the Main Overlook. The accessible walkway shortly intersects the Grandview Rim Trail, which leaves left and is your return route. Stay straight toward the Main Overlook, passing the Tunnel Trail leaving right, and the Castle Rock Trail, leaving left. Just ahead come to the Main Overlook. This fenced sandstone slab presents stellar views into the brawling river canyon below. Backtrack just a bit and then pick up the Castle Rock Trail, heading north-bound below the rim of the gorge on a singletrack rocky path.

- **0.2** Come along a steep cliff line rising to your left. The cliff line continues more often than not, forming a castle-like wall that gives the trail its name.

- **0.7** Meet the Grandview Rim Trail. Turn left, joining the developed path southbound through rhododendron, now atop the bluff. The walking is much easier.

0.8 After passing a spur leading right to Picnic Shelter #1, turn acutely left toward the North Overlook. Views open of the gorge below, especially the mining town of Quinnimont, and the rapids nearby that are named for the place where coal was first mined from the New River Gorge. After enjoying the views from North Overlook, backtrack to rejoin the Grandview Rim Trail southbound.

1.0 Another spur trail leads right to the park amphitheater. Keep straight on the edge of the gorge rim in upland hardwoods. Enter the manicured part of Grandview.

1.2 Complete the hike after finishing the Grandview Rim Trail and then joining the stone path to arrive back at the parking area and trailhead.

15 Glade Creek Trail

Take a walk up one of the New River Gorge's larger wild tributaries. Start your hike near the old village site of Hamlet, worth a side exploration. The Glade Creek Trail takes you up an untamed valley on a foot-friendly path. After a mile, reach a huge pool fed by a charming waterfall. Continue in rich woods, where wildflowers proliferate in spring. Look for old settler relics in flats. Trout-filled pools beckon anglers along this catch-and-release stream. Reach a footbridge crossing the stream. It presents good water views and a turnaround point.

Distance: 6.2-mile there-and-back

Hiking time: About 3.0 to 4.0 hours

Difficulty: More difficult due to distance

Trail surface: Crushed gravel and natural surface

Best season: Spring for wildflowers and waterfalls

Other trail users: None

Canine compatibility: Leashed dogs permitted

Fees and permits: None

Schedule: 24/7/365

Maps: Trail Areas of New River Gorge; USGS Prince

Trail contacts: New River Gorge National Park and Preserve, 104 Main St., Glen Jean 25846; (304) 465-0508; www.nps.gov/neri

Finding the trailhead: From exit 124 on I-64 east of Beckley, take the Beckley Bypass north for 1 mile, and then stay straight at a traffic light, reaching Stanaford Road at 2.2 miles from the interstate. Turn right on Stanaford Road, WV 41 north. Follow Stanaford Road for 4.4 miles, and then turn right at a stop sign and the intersection with WV 61. Stay with WV 41 north for 3.8 miles, descending into the New River Gorge. Stay right with Glade Creek Road just before WV 41 crosses the New River via a bridge. Trace Glade Creek Road for 5.6 miles to a dead end. The trailhead is on your right, as a short spur heads left to Glade Creek Campground. GPS trailhead coordinates: 37.827212, -81.010663

The Hike

Glade Creek Valley is a jewel of the New River Gorge National Park and Preserve. The lower 6 miles of this tributary are part of the protected national park. It encompasses a large watershed that includes a historic townsite, a trout-fishing stream, a campground, and a set of hiking trails. This particular hike explores the stream valley from near its confluence with the New River to a bridge upstream.

Follow the old railroad grade deep into impressive tall woodland. Preserved hemlocks complement deciduous trees that display copious color in autumn. Steep slopes rise from the valley floor. Fallen boulders occupy the stream and forest. On Glade Creek alluring translucent aquamarine pools alternate with melodic shoals.

An ideal swimming hole and 10-foot Glade Creek Falls are located 1.0 mile into the hike. The pool far outstrips the waterfall in size, but the scene is a good one in its entirety. From the swimming hole you can see the trail ahead was built up with a creekside floodwall. Continue enjoying picturesque valley sweeps while heading up Glade Creek. Pass occasional campsites in flats. You may also see old relics from homesites in these areas. The trail grade remains moderate except where it has to work around rockslides that have fallen over the path. After 3.0 miles, come to an arched bridge spanning Glade Creek. It makes a good stopping spot and still leaves you 3.0 miles of hiking back to the trailhead. Intrepid aggressive hikers will continue on 1.7 miles to

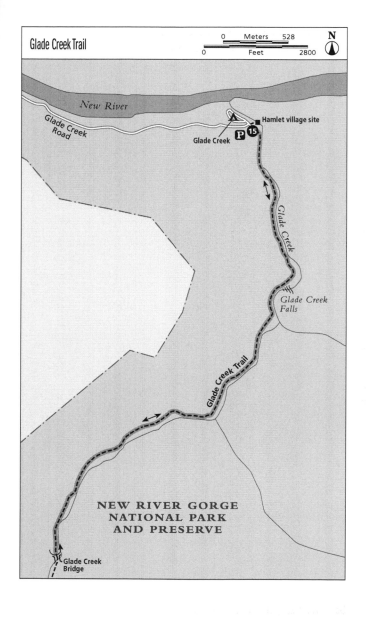

Glade Creek Trail

0   Meters   528
0   Feet   2800

N

New River

Glade Creek Road

Hamlet village site

Glade Creek

P 15

Glade Creek

Glade Creek Falls

Glade Creek Trail

NEW RIVER GORGE
NATIONAL PARK
AND PRESERVE

Glade Creek Bridge

25-foot Kates Branch Falls, located on a tributary of Glade Creek.

Consider staying at the Glade Creek Campground while here. It stands underneath thick and towering woodland of locust, river birch, buckeye, sycamore, and tulip trees. Five campsites are strung along a gravel road. A picnic table, fire ring, and lantern post adorn each flat spot. Five riverfront walk-in tent sites lie on a beach near the New River boat launch. Park your car and walk down the sandbar, shaded in river birch and sycamore, and pick one of the five marked campsites. The campsites are free of charge.

Hikers can also enjoy the Kates Plateau and Polls Plateau Trails, connecting to the Glade Creek Trail up from this hike's end. In addition to hiking, visitors to Glade Creek like to bank fish or get on the New River in jon boats for the numerous smallmouth bass. The swimming is good in the river, but life jackets are recommended by the park service. There is a solid current.

Another way to get on the New River is by kayak, canoe, or raft. The section of river from Hinton to Thurmond is Class I–II with a few Class III rapids. You can and should portage around two rough but pretty spots, Brooks Falls and Sandstone Falls. The 5-mile run from Glade Creek to Grandview Sandbar is a popular and convenient paddle from this campground. And don't forget to explore Hamlet; the townsite is across the railroad bridge from the trailhead parking area. Remember to leave any artifacts you might find.

Miles and Directions

0.0 Take the marked trail heading upstream along the right bank of Glade Creek. The pedestrian bridge crossing over Glade Creek leads to the village site of Hamlet. Hamlet is worth exploring, but many people confuse this with the beginning of the Glade Creek Trail. Instead, trace a gravel path upstream, which soon gets pinched in by a landslide on your right. A large pool lies below this landslide. The trail narrows.

0.9 The trail and creek make a big bend to the right.

1.0 Come to a huge pool beneath 10-foot Glade Creek Falls. This is a popular swimming hole.

2.0 Leave the railroad grade, working around an old rockslide.

3.1 Reach the arched bridge over Glade Creek, located at the head of a large wooded flat. Turn around here.

6.2 Arrive back at the Glade Creek Trailhead.

16 Little Beaver State Park Hike

Enjoy a circuit through scenic forest at a West Virginia state park situated on a tributary of the New River. Start along Laurel Run at a pretty picnic area and make your way up the Laurel Run Valley in a lush forest. Walk among rhododendron and towering hardwoods on the mostly level trail, and then turn down an old railroad grade. Pass a homesite before completing the trek. Laurel Run provides aquatic beauty throughout the jaunt. Little Beaver Lake, a fine campground, and other trails make this park a relaxing, natural getaway.

Distance: 2.1-mile loop
Hiking time: About 1.5 to 2.5 hours
Difficulty: Moderate; does have rocky trail bed
Trail surface: Natural surface
Best season: Year-round
Other trail users: A few bikers
Canine compatibility: Leashed dogs permitted

Fees and permits: None
Schedule: Sunrise to sunset
Maps: Little Beaver State Park Map & Trail Guide; USGS Prince
Trail contacts: Little Beaver State Park, 1402 Grandview Rd., Beaver 25813; (304) 763-2494; www.littlebeaverstatepark.com

Finding the trailhead: From exit 129 on I-64 east of Beckley, take WV 9, Grandview Road, south away from the interstate. Stay straight for Shady Grove as the road becomes WV 307 east at 0.3 mile. Stay with WV 307 east for 1.3 more miles to the park entrance on your left. Enter the state park and immediately pass the park office on your right. After 0.1 mile turn right then immediately turn left into the picnic area parking. Park at the upper end of the parking area, near the footpath accessing Picnic Shelter #3. GPS trailhead coordinates: 37.754200, -81.076217

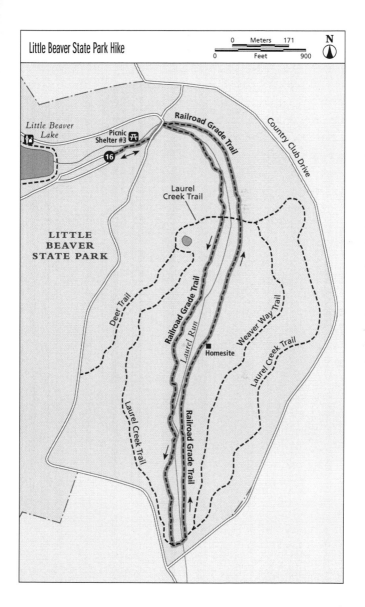

Little Beaver State Park Hike

0   Meters   171
0   Feet   900

N

Little Beaver Lake

Picnic Shelter #3

Railroad Grade Trail

Country Club Drive

Laurel Creek Trail

LITTLE BEAVER STATE PARK

Deer Trail

Railroad Grade Trail

Laurel Run

Homesite

Weaver Way Trail

Laurel Creek Trail

Laurel Creek Trail

Railroad Grade Trail

The Hike

Little Beaver State Park is located on the upper watershed of Little Beaver Creek. This stream flows into Beaver Creek, which flows into Piney Creek, which flows into the New River near Prince. The 562-acre park is centered by 18-acre Little Beaver Lake, which offers quality fishing for trout, catfish, and bass. You can also explore the lake on self-propelled watercraft, available for rent. Five picnic shelters avail scenic outdoor dining locations. The preserve also features a fine campground. But it may have more trails than anything. Over 20 miles of paths form an extensive trail network that covers almost the entire landscape.

This hike is one of the more scenic ones, as it explores the Laurel Run Valley and is primarily used by hikers. Many of the other trails are popular with mountain bikers. But the rocky footbed of the Railroad Grade Trail keeps most of the rubber tire set on other paths. Don't be daunted by the stony trail, for hikers can easily put their feet in the right place untroubled by the rocks.

The hike uses the trail accessing Picnic Shelter #3 to reach the Railroad Grade Trail. Laurel Run gurgles over rocks and beneath scads of rhododendron. The thickets of rhododendron likely gave this creek its name, for historically mountaineers referred to rhododendron as "laurel." Just to confuse matters further, they called mountain laurel "ivy." Name aside, this rhododendron will sport its white-and-pink blooms in the summertime. Layers of vegetation rise above the Railroad Grade Trail. White pines tower above all, and then comes a layer of moisture-tolerant hardwoods such as black birch and Fraser magnolia. Rhododendron remains the primary undergrowth, though mosses and ferns occupy wetter areas. You are not on an old railroad grade yet, but rather a winding footpath.

Laurel Run tumbles in pools and shoals amid rocks. The trail remains nearly level despite its heading up the cool stream valley. Elevation changes on this circuit are less than 100 feet between high and low point. The trail and creek wind in unison. Step over intermittent tributaries. The loop crosses Laurel Run at a trail junction and then begins its journey back downstream on the wider, more level, yet stony railroad grade.

Ahead, the trail meets an old homesite, easily identified by a rock wall to the right of the path. The straight nature of the old railroad grade allows for distant looks through rich woodland. In places the ground was elevated to keep the railroad grade level; in yet other situations hillsides were blasted, keeping the elevation changes of the railroad track manageable. Enter flatter terrain, working past tributaries. The valley widens before reaching the campground access road. From here it is but a short backtrack to finish the hike.

Miles and Directions

0.0 Pick up the footpath leading toward Picnic Shelter #3. Soon pass the wooden structure and continue uphill with Laurel Run flowing to your left.

0.1 Reach the campground access road. Turn left here, carefully walking along the paved roadway to intersect the Railroad Grade Trail. You will see two accesses for the Railroad Grade Trail. Take the first one you reach, heading upstream with Laurel Run flowing on your left.

0.4 Intersect the Laurel Creek Trail (this is the name of the trail despite the official name of the creek being Laurel Run). It leaves right and forms a loop in the upper bowl of the Laurel

Run valley. Pass on your right a clearing whose vegetation is growing back.

0.9 Walk under a transmission line.

1.0 Intersect the Laurel Creek Trail again. It leaves right and left. Stay left here to bridge Laurel Run. Just after going over Laurel Run, immediately turn left with the Railroad Grade Trail. The Laurel Creek Trail heads away, intersecting the Weaver Way Trail. You have now officially joined the railroad grade for which the path is named. It was used in long-ago logging operations. Pass back under the power line.

1.3 Come near the rock wall of an old homesite, now covered with white pines. Continue down the evergreen alley of Laurel Run.

1.7 Cross the Laurel Creek Trail a final time.

2.0 Return to the campground access road. Turn left here and begin backtracking.

2.1 Arrive back at the trailhead after passing Picnic Area #3.

17 Gwinn Ridge Trail

This trail oozes solitude. If you are looking to escape the crowds on a busy weekend or simply enjoy a private commune with nature, this is the hike for you. Gwinn Ridge is a lonely mountain north of Hinton around which the New River flows, dividing Brooks Falls from Sandstone Falls. However, you will be walking nearly a thousand feet above the New River, traversing woods transitioning from fields where a hardscrabble farm once existed. The interface between meadow and forest makes for ample wildlife viewing. A keen eye will also spot relics from the days when Gwinn Ridge was inhabited.

Distance: 3.2-mile loop
Hiking time: About 2.0 to 3.0 hours
Difficulty: Moderate; does have 250-foot elevation change
Trail surface: Natural surface
Best season: Fall for colors, avoid late summer
Other trail users: None
Canine compatibility: Leashed dogs permitted

Fees and permits: None
Schedule: 24/7/365
Maps: Trail Areas of New River Gorge; USGS Hinton
Trail contacts: New River Gorge National Park and Preserve, 104 Main St., Glen Jean 25846; (304) 465-0508; www.nps.gov/neri

Finding the trailhead: From exit 139 on I-64 east of Beckley, take WV 20 south for 5.8 miles to gravel Brooks Mountain Road. Turn left on Brooks Mountain Road and follow it 2.3 miles to the trailhead on your left, in a gap. Alternate directions: From the town square in Hinton, take WV 20 north for 4.5 miles to Brooks Mountain Road and

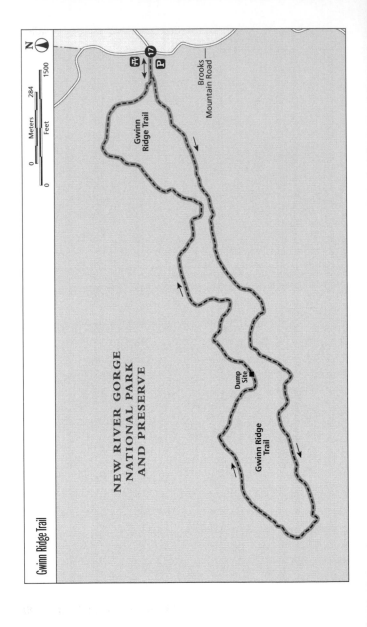

Gwinn Ridge Trail

NEW RIVER GORGE
NATIONAL PARK
AND PRESERVE

Gwinn Ridge Trail

Gwinn Ridge Trail

Dump Site

Brooks Mountain Road

N

0   Meters   284

0   Feet   1500

turn left, and then follow the above directions. GPS trailhead coordinates: 37.749000, -80.890783

The Hike

This is seemingly the forgotten trail of the New River Gorge National Park and Preserve. It is off the beaten path and doesn't have a singular feature that draws hikers to it. I find it a worthy hike and hope you will too. The Gwinn Ridge Trail takes you to a place that progress has left behind, a place where nature is recapturing what once was a farm. Gwinn Ridge stands at about 2,400 feet and is part of a wider swath of the mostly narrow 70,000 acres that make up the New River Gorge National Park and Preserve, run by the National Park Service. The national park and preserve was established in 1978, and over time open lands like this have returned from field to forest. In other places old homes and homesites have also faded into the rising trees. However, the park has preserved many other historic locales. Several hikes in this guide visit such locales. But Gwinn Ridge is being left to the deer and bear, both of which you may see on your hike.

A shaded picnic table stands adjacent to the trailhead. Interestingly, across the road from the trailhead is the Three Rivers Avian Center, a place where injured raptors are rehabilitated. They aid in the recovery of falcons, eagles, owls, and hawks. The center also offers outreach programs specializing in environmental education. To learn about the programs please visit www.tracwv.org, perhaps timing your hike with a visit to the avian center.

Much of the hike will be on old roadbeds used by former residents. This makes the hiking easy, though brush may overtake the trail in late summer. Strategically placed arrows keep you on the correct path. Young deciduous hardwoods such as tulip trees, red maple, and locust crowd the trail. Grass rises in open areas during the warm season. Blackberries will ripen in summer. Pine, cedar, and sumac trees find their place as well. Look for old fencerows and also trees growing in distinct lines, all evidence of past agricultural use. The path remains level for a good way, allowing you to soak in the surroundings. An unnamed tributary to the south cuts a 1,200-foot drop to the New River. Small persistent clearings open to your right. This was the top of the ridge, a tableland, and the flattest place for agriculture. Gwinn Ridge spurs off greater Chestnut Mountain.

Limited gorge views open to your left as the New curves around this ridge. These views will be enhanced during leaf-off, as will your ability to spot settler evidence. In places, straight, gray-trunked tulip trees almost single-handedly dominate the forest. Their leaves turn a bright yellow in fall. Wildflowers, ferns, and other trees become more numerous as the trail descends, and then doubles back and turns easterly around the north side of the ridge. The trail bed becomes very rocky.

It isn't long before you return to the ridgetop and the site of where the forgotten farmer tossed his trash. You can see broken farm implements, glass bottles, and such. There was no garbage service up here. Residents simply burned up what they could and tossed the rest. Continue along the brow of the ridge. Wintertime views open. Note the club moss at your feet. It grows thick in disturbed sites. After passing under a power line, the trail surprisingly drops off the ridge once more. After reaching a low point, the path turns up a hollow, closing out the loop. It is but 200 feet back to the trailhead, ending the hike.

Miles and Directions

0.0 Leave the trailhead, heading westerly on an old roadbed. The loop portion of the hike begins a couple of hundred feet from the trailhead. Split left here.

0.4 Pass under a power-line clearing.

1.0 The trail turns sharply right.

1.1 The path begins to descend. Drop off the ridgetop into higher canopied forest.

1.4 The trail makes a pair of switchbacks on a mid-slope flat. Curve to the north side of Gwinn Ridge.

1.8 Begin ascending to the ridgetop and formerly settled terrain.

2.0 Stay left on the ridgetop. Pass the dump site of former residents.

2.6 Walk back under the power line, and then pick up an old roadbed dropping sharply left.

3.2 Complete the loop, arriving back at the trailhead after rising a final time to the ridge.

18 Sandstone Falls

This is your chance to visit the undisputed most powerful waterfall in the New River Gorge and all of West Virginia. Sandstone Falls spans 1,500 feet across the New River as it makes picturesque drops ranging from 10 to 25 feet. Start by crossing the channel of an old gristmill on an all-access boardwalk, then view horseshoe-shaped Lower Falls. From there continue on the boardwalk to bridge an island and view the Main Falls. The last part of the hike circles an island where you can walk alongside the New River as well as the oft-dammed-by-beavers gristmill channel.

Distance: 1.1-mile balloon loop
Hiking time: About 1.0 hour
Difficulty: Easy
Trail surface: Natural surface and boardwalk
Best season: Winter through spring for boldest falls
Other trail users: None
Canine compatibility: Leashed dogs permitted

Fees and permits: None
Schedule: Sunrise to sunset
Maps: Trails Areas of New River Gorge; USGS Hinton
Trail contacts: New River Gorge National Park and Preserve, 104 Main St., Glen Jean 25846; (304) 465-0508; www.nps.gov/neri

Finding the trailhead: From the town square in Hinton, take WV 20 south across the bridge over the New River. Immediately after the bridge, turn right on River Road/CR 26 and follow it for 8 miles to the Sandstone Falls parking area on your right. GPS trailhead coordinates: 37.759261, -80.905380

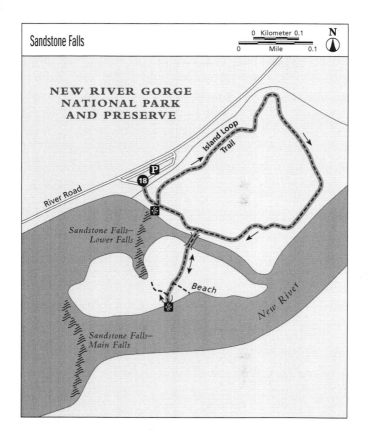

Sandstone Falls

NEW RIVER GORGE
NATIONAL PARK
AND PRESERVE

River Road

Island Loop Trail

P

18

Sandstone Falls—
Lower Falls

Beach

New River

Sandstone Falls—
Main Falls

The Hike

This is one powerful rumbler, stretching 1,500 feet wide
from bank to bank on the mighty New River. Sandstone
Falls drops anywhere from 10 to 25 feet vertically along
two primary drops—Main Falls and Lower Falls—that are
divided by a series of islands.

You will see evidence of this formidable flow in multiple ways on this walk. First, you will follow the Sandstone Falls Boardwalk across the channel once used by the Richmond clan who built a gristmill here, harnessing the power of moving water to grind wheat and corn for neighbors and customers. Next, you will see Lower Falls and the thundering curtain of white, inexorably weathering away rock while cutting the valley ever deeper. You will then cross a bridge to an island that offers a view of the Main Falls where even more water roars over the shelf of sandstone, causing clouds of mist to rise from the base of the cataract. This first part of the hike uses a boardwalk that makes for easy travel for waterfall enthusiasts of all ages and abilities.

The second part of the hike uses the Island Loop Trail to circle through what is known as an Appalachian Riverside Flatrock Community—a special habitat found only on big Appalachian waterways that experience regular flooding. Here, intermittent cataclysmic inundations sweep across islands such as this, stripping the sandstone base, leaving plants in a constant survival and succession pattern where lichens create soil, then moss and small plants grow followed by scrub pines, post oak, and cedars, only to have the risen trees swept away by floods. And the process starts over again.

The walk is one of the gorge's finest. From the two overlooks of Lower Falls, not only will you see this curved cataract but also unbelievable amounts of trapped timber—and I mean whole trees—that have floated the river and gotten stuck in the warm-up rapids above Sandstone Falls. In the background, mountains rise majestically toward the sky, clad in luxuriant forests. The quarter-mile width of the river cuts a widespread swath as you look upstream. It is a true combination of power, size, and grandeur. The primary overlook of Main Falls delivers a more distant perspective. This white froth rumbles like a train. Field glasses will help you appreciate it better, but even from this lengthy vantage the might of Main Falls is unmistakable.

While on the hike look for beaver evidence and the wetlands they have created, yet another part of the mosaic of wonderment that is greater Sandstone Falls.

Miles and Directions

0.0 Join the Sandstone Falls Boardwalk to immediately bridge the channel along which the Richmond gristmill was built. Join an unnamed island. The other end of the Island Loop Trail leaves left and is your return route. For the moment, keep straight on the boardwalk.

0.1 Come to the first developed overlook of Lower Falls, the more northerly cataract of greater Sandstone Falls. This falls tumbles in horseshoe fashion between the mainland and an island in the river. Ahead, reach a second overlook of Lower Falls. Continuing past this second overlook you come to a trail intersection. Here, Island Loop Trail keeps straight as a natural surface path, while the Sandstone Falls Boardwalk leaves right on an impressive iron truss bridge. For now, stay with boardwalk, spanning the iron truss bridge. Look upstream for a straight-on look at Lower Falls.

0.2 Follow the boardwalk on to yet another island after crossing the iron truss bridge. To your left, a short path drops left to a sandy beach. Keep straight on the boardwalk after visiting the beach, then circle around a sandstone rock upthrust to emerge at a developed viewpoint of the Main Falls. Here, you can look upstream a good distance at the wide and loud spiller, the largest in all of West Virginia. After viewing Main Falls, return to cross the iron truss bridge and then head right on the Island Loop.

0.3 Join the Island Loop Trail, returning almost to the trailhead then making a clockwise circuit. Hike through rising forest heavy with sycamore. Note the debris piled up against the bases of trees, left there during high water events.

0.5 Come alongside the New River. Enjoy another close-up look at the massive waterway, bordered with sand and shells.

0.6 Turn away from the river. Cruise through woods.

0.8 Come alongside the former gristmill canal channel and turn upstream.

1.1 Complete the Island Loop Trail and turn right, crossing the gristmill channel to reach the trailhead.

19 Big Branch Loop

Start this hike at attractive Brooks Falls, a cataract on the New River. From this water feature complemented with a picnic area, hike up Big Branch, a steep and intimate tributary of the New. Work your way up the wildflower-filled vale, passing small cascades before reaching an old homesite and a pair of waterfalls. From here the trail traverses wooded hillsides before making its way back down to the New River.

Distance: 2.1-mile loop
Hiking time: About 1.5 to 2.0 hours
Difficulty: Moderate; does have a solid climb
Trail surface: Natural surface
Best season: Spring for wildflowers, winter for views
Other trail users: None
Canine compatibility: Leashed dogs permitted

Fees and permits: None
Schedule: Sunrise to sunset
Maps: Trail Areas of New River Gorge; USGS Hinton
Trail contacts: New River Gorge National Park and Preserve, 104 Main St., Glen Jean 25846; (304) 465-0508; www.nps.gov/neri

Finding the trailhead: From the town square in Hinton, take WV 20 south across the bridge over the New River. Immediately after the bridge, turn right on River Road/CR 26 and follow it for 4 miles to the Brooks Falls Picnic Area on your right. The Big Branch Trail starts at the turn into the picnic area, away from the river. GPS trailhead coordinates: 37.717022, -80.893238

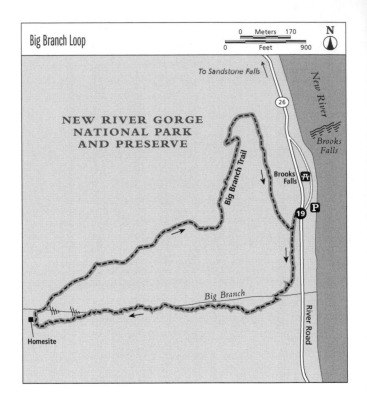

0 Meters 170
0 Feet 900

N

To Sandstone Falls

NEW RIVER GORGE
NATIONAL PARK
AND PRESERVE

New River

26

Brooks
Falls

Big Branch Trail

Brooks
Falls

19 P

Big Branch

River Road

Homesite

The Hike

Make sure and allow time to enjoy the trailhead scenery. Here you will gain a close-up view of Brooks Falls, a long Class III rapid. Near the trailhead, the rapid has begun falling in innumerable chutes and channels. As you walk along the lower picnic area, the rapids increase and culminate in a final drop. The final drop itself is just a few feet, but casual paddlers should portage this. Low sandstone cliffs adjoining the picnic area allow for excellent views of this rapid. Speaking of picnicking, hikers should certainly add a riverside meal to their adventure. Also, Sandstone Falls, generally claimed to be 25 feet in height and the New River's highest fall, is just a few miles down the road and could be a worthy side trip.

This hike, however, takes the Big Branch Trail, leaving the wide, open New River to enter full-blown forest on a slender trail. The woods are thick and lush on this gorge slope, with vines interwoven into bountiful deciduous trees. The rocky, rooty trail eases along the mountainside and then turns south, aiming for Big Branch. Rocky, intermittent streambeds flow off the mountainside and cross the path. The rumble of Brooks Falls lessens as you reach Big Branch. Sure, Big Branch makes its own noise as it spills from Swell Mountain above, but it seems a mere kitten's purr compared to the lion's roar of the New River cutting its way to meet the Gauley River downstream, forming the Kanawha River that flows through Charleston to meet the Ohio River.

Buckeye, sycamore, and cherry thrive in this moist, ferny vale, which can be suffocatingly humid in summer. Moss grows on anything that doesn't move. Stinging nettle breeds dense by late summer. In spring you will find a cornucopia of wildflowers, from violets to trilliums and more. The trail works its way up the slender defile, crisscrossing the creek in places. These crossings will be easy to negotiate, save for flood conditions. Big Branch descends in attractive ledge drops divided by shallow pools as it dives steeply to meet the New River. There are bountiful small cascades but no significant waterfall until farther upstream. Watch for small bluffs and rock overhangs uphill from the trail.

The ascent continues. In winter you may be able to see piled rocks off to your left where the declivitous mountainside was cleared for pasturage. Even the most recalcitrant

Appalachian subsistence farmer couldn't have hoed corn on this part of Big Branch. Ahead, the valley does level off enough for a solitude-loving hillbilly to have established a homestead. You will see the rock wall of the site just before crossing over Big Branch a final time. Though cursed with rocky soil and a remote site, the residents of this locale were blessed with a pair of waterfalls below their residence.

From here, the loop climbs into distinctly different dry hardwood forest. The echo of songbirds rings across the hills. The trail joins a rib ridge before turning into an intermittent streambed. Here it makes a loping curve deeper into the lower New River Gorge. The descent is continuous, and you soon are back at Brooks Falls.

Miles and Directions

0.0 Pick up the singletrack Big Branch Trail at the upper end of the Brooks Falls Picnic Area. Quickly come to the loop portion of the hike. Split left, southbound.

0.2 Turn into the Big Branch watershed. Step over the creek and join an old wagon track heading up the valley.

0.4 The trail steepens. Crisscross the creek.

0.7 Reach Lower Big Branch Falls, a 20-foot sheet drop over a mossy angled ledge.

0.8 Reach the rock wall of an old homesite on your left. Just ahead cross Big Branch above 15-foot Upper Big Branch Falls. In late summer this cascade will be but a trickle.

1.0 Level off in xeric hardwoods. The walking is easy.

1.2 Pass under a power line. Curve around a point. The roar of the New River rises.

1.4 Begin the big drop. Turn into a shallow hollow.

1.6 The river bluff is nearly vertical. Winter views open wide.

2.1 Complete the loop and walk just a few feet back to the trail-head.

20 Bluestone Turnpike

This old river road–turned–trail travels the corridor along the Bluestone National Wild and Scenic River, a tributary of the New River. The mostly level trek provides expansive views of the Bluestone River, making its way past bluffs and rich forests en route to the townsite of Lilly, where the Bluestone and the Little Bluestone Rivers meet. Your return hike will yield not only more natural splendor but also more traces of human history.

Distance: 4.2-mile there-and-back

Hiking time: About 2.5 to 3.5 hours

Difficulty: Moderate

Trail surface: Natural surface

Best season: Year-round

Other trail users: Equestrians, bikers

Canine compatibility: Leashed dogs permitted

Fees and permits: None

Schedule: Sunrise to sunset

Maps: Bluestone State Park; USGS Pipestem

Trail contacts: Bluestone National Scenic River, PO Box 246, 104 Main St., Glen Jean 25846; (304) 465-0508; www.nps.gov/blue

Finding the trailhead: From the town square in Hinton, take WV 20 south for 5.2 miles to the right turn to Bluestone State Park. Follow the main entrance road for 2.1 miles to the park office. From here angle left toward the Old Mill Campground. Trace this park road for 1.8 miles more to dead-end at the trailhead, shortly after passing the left turn into Old Mill Campground. GPS trailhead coordinates: 37.602379, -80.946284

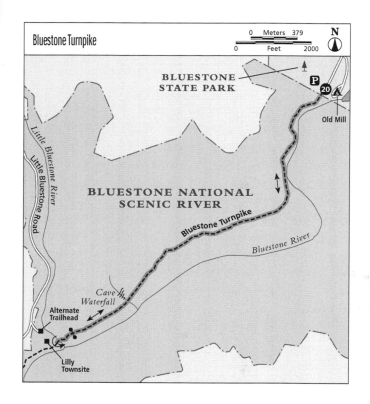

Meters 379

Feet 2000

N

BLUESTONE
STATE PARK

P
20

Old Mill

Little Bluestone River

Little Bluestone Road

BLUESTONE NATIONAL
SCENIC RIVER

Bluestone Turnpike

Bluestone River

*Cave
Waterfall*

Alternate
Trailhead

Lilly
Townsite

The Hike

The Bluestone Turnpike connects two different West Virginia state parks—Bluestone State Park and Pipestem State Park, on land managed by the National Park Service. A century back this old road was used by farmers, fishermen, and other residents of this deep river valley, a major tributary of the New River. Bluestone Dam, completed in 1949, rises just downstream of the Bluestone River and the New River's confluence. Residents of the lower Bluestone River valley were forced to leave their homes, emptying an already sparsely populated gorge. Originally engineers estimated the height of the lake created by Bluestone Dam to be higher than what ended up, leaving the lower Bluestone River free-flowing and in federal ownership. With its plant diversity and thousand-foot-deep gorge, the Bluestone River became a candidate for Wild and Scenic status.

The Bluestone Turnpike stays on the west side of the river the entire hike. Initially the river isn't visible. However, the trail rises a bit to a bluff, presenting an elevated vista of musical rapids, gravel bars, big boulders, and islands. This portion of the waterway offers mild whitewater, but only during late winter and spring, when it is high enough to be floated. In summer and fall the Bluestone flows more placidly and is used by anglers and swimmers.

The entire trail is 8 miles one way. Interestingly, you can take a tram from Pipestem State Park down to the southerly trailhead or connect to it using other hiking trails. The northern end has a more modest beginning. Simply follow the old roadbed, noting the blasted walls that created this transportation corridor through this rugged defile. Area residents moved themselves and their goods along what is now a recreational path we can enjoy. Oak, maple, and other hardwoods rise on hills above, with moist species such as sycamore, ash, river birch, buckeye, and pawpaw holding sway near the river. Wildflowers will color the valley from spring through fall.

You will cross several rocky tributaries of the Bluestone River en route to the townsite of Lilly. Most of the streams will be dry, save for spring and after heavy rains. Natural bluffs stand high above the trail. Upon reaching the townsite of Lilly, make sure and explore. Lilly came to be in the late

1700s and was occupied until the mid-1900s, one of the first European habitations in what came to be West Virginia. Home foundations, a cemetery, and other evidence awaits. Also, head down to the confluence of the Bluestone and Little Bluestone Rivers. It's a scenic spot. A large pool lies upstream of this confluence. Once you have had your fill, retrace your steps for the 2.1 miles back to where you started.

Miles and Directions

0.0 Pass around a pole gate, heading southbound on the Bluestone Turnpike.

0.3 Come directly alongside the Bluestone River.

0.4 Pass on your right a clearing whose vegetation is regrowing.

0.6 The trail and river become separated by a large wooded flat.

1.4 Step over a perennial stream.

1.7 Look right for a spring forming a waterfall below the mouth of the cave.

2.0 Pass around another pole gate. A spur leads left to the river.

2.1 Bridge the Little Bluestone River and reach the town of Lilly. A spur trail leads right to the alternate trailhead. Explore the townsite, and then backtrack.

4.2 Arrive back at the Bluestone State Park trailhead.

About the Author

Johnny Molloy is an outdoor adventurer and writer based in Johnson City, Tennessee. His outdoor passion started on a backpacking trip in Great Smoky Mountains National Park while attending the University of Tennessee. That first foray unleashed a love of the outdoors that has led the Tennessee native to spending most of his time backpacking, canoe camping, and tent camping for the past three decades.

Friends enjoyed his outdoor adventure stories; one even suggested he write a book. He pursued his friend's idea and soon parlayed his love of the outdoors into an occupation. The result of his efforts is more than eighty-five books and guides. His writings include hiking, camping, and paddling guidebooks; comprehensive guidebooks about specific areas; and true outdoor adventure books covering the eastern United States.

He continues writing and traveling extensively throughout the United States, endeavoring in a variety of outdoor pursuits. A Christian, Johnny is an active member of Christ Community Church in Johnson City, as well as being a Gideon. His non-outdoor interests include reading, American history, and University of Tennessee sports. For the latest on Johnny, please visit www.johnnymolloy.com.